I'LL NEVER WALK ALONE

I'LL NEVER WALK ALONE

AN AUTOBIOGRAPHY

GERRY MARSDEN

with RAY COLEMAN

BLOOMSBURY

Friday March '65

FERRY Cross The Mersey. ✱

INTRO:- De —— Da De Do Do, Da - De Do Do SLIDE BASS STay
From B DOWN to E open

Life goes on DAy AFTER DAY
Hearts Torn in' Every - way So
Ferry Cross The Mersey Cos This Lands The Place I Love
AND here I'll STAY

(✱ Just iN
CASE)

~~People with love every where~~ ✱

People they Rush everywhere
EAch with their own ~~secret~~ CARE
So Ferry Cross The Mersey and Always take me There
the PLACE I Love.

People AROUND Every corner
~~Seem~~ to Smile ' and Say
~~We Don't care where you come from~~ ✱
We Don't care What Your Name is But
We'll Never Turn You Away

✱

So I'll Continue to Say
'Here I Always will Stay
So Ferry Cross The Mersey Cos This Lands
AND Here I'll Stay. the Place I Love
" " " " " END KEY oF. E SLOW.
Fairely

'Ferry Cross the Mersey', 1965: my early handwritten
draft of the lyrics for a song about Liverpool and its
people that became special all over the world.

First published in Great Britain 1993
Bloomsbury Publishing Limited, 2 Soho Square, London W1V 5DE

Copyright © 1993 by Gerry Marsden and Ray Coleman

The moral right of the authors has been asserted

Lyric on page 59 from 'You'll Never Walk Alone'
by Rodgers & Hammerstein © Hal Leonard Publishing Corporation, USA

A CIP catalogue record for this book
is available from the British Library

ISBN 0 7475 1473 9

Typeset by Hewer Text Composition Services, Edinburgh

For Pauline and our daughters Yvette and Vicky
. . . with love and thanks for getting me through it!

CONTENTS

PICTURE SOURCES

Disc: page 5 *bottom*
Carl Fox: page 12 *bottom*
Harry Goodwin: pages 1 *bottom*, 15 *bottom left & right*
Hastings Printing Company: pages 8 *bottom*, 10 *top left & right*
Tom Hustler: pages 10 *bottom*, 11 *bottom*
Dick James Music Limited: page 4 *bottom*
Peter Kaye: page 3 *middle*
Kaye Photography: page 2 *top right*
David Kendall: page 13 *middle*
Keystone Press Agency: page 6 *middle*
Joe Matthews: page 11 *top*
National Screen Service Corporation: page 7 *top right*
Nems Enterprises Limited: page 5 *middle*
Newspix: page 6 *middle*
David Redfern/Redferns: page 14 *middle*
Rex Features Limited: page 5 *top*
Souvenir: page 7 *top left*
Star-Club: page 3 *top & bottom*
R. J. Stephens: page 2 *top left*
United Artists: page 8 *top*
Ann Wilson: page 7 *bottom*
Lloyd Wright: page 14 *bottom*

Preface

In the 1960s he was the cocky Liverpudlian with an infectious grin, some hearty and hummable pop songs and a wacky sense of humour. On and off stage he could be cutting but not malicious, and he always had that endearing Merseyside characteristic of smiling through any adversity. He also possessed iron determination.

In the 1990s, Gerry Marsden is, not surprisingly, the same man. Three decades of success have scarcely changed him. His music, his personality and above all his spirit embody the qualities that have made the sounds of Liverpool so lasting and so celebrated. Gerry belonged to an era when his music was known generically as pop rather than rock, and pop (as in popular) it has remained.

He was the second act (after the Beatles) to be signed to management by Brian Epstein, and Epstein correctly forecast that Gerry would eventually step beyond pop music into the fields of cabaret, film and theatre. Behind Gerry's casual smile was a conviction that he was going to be in show business for life, and that he would justify Epstein's faith. And he did exactly that.

Today, celebrating thirty years since he scored three direct number one hits in quick succession in 1963, Gerry is an established success as a world-travelling entertainer. And as the legendary status of the 1960s and its stars grows ever stronger, so does the reputation of one of its most famous sons. He has moved beyond music: from his stage he spreads his personality of wit, warmth and that infectious smile that is his trademark.

We first met in 1963, a heady year in which the axis of popular culture shifted from London to Liverpool and then travelled the globe. It was my good fortune at that crucial time to be a writer with the *Melody Maker*, a London music paper. We looked with some disdain on this weird invading army of young 'beat group' guitarists and pioneering songwriters from faraway Liverpool who were gradually taking control of the best-selling record charts (which were then called the 'hit parade').

The year 1963, when Gerry Marsden scored his impact, was one of profound change on the world stage. In Britain, Sir Alec Douglas-Home succeeded Harold Macmillan as Prime Minister. Television's famous Saturday night satire programme 'That Was The Week That Was', launching David Frost, was making its mark. Britain was refused entry into the European Economic Community. Harold Wilson was elected leader of the Labour Party. And the unemployment figure, at 878,356, was at its highest since 1947.

In America, President John F. Kennedy was assassinated. On 1 June, Pope John XXIII died. The space race had begun: Russia had sent up the first woman astronaut and the French had sent a cat, both returning safely.

Gerry and the Pacemakers' optimistic music was part of the soundtrack of those years. Gerry Marsden was a terrier-like follow-up to the first impact by the Beatles – and he lost no time in telling me that he was not riding their coat tails. Liverpool was ablaze with great groups, he said at the time; he and the 'Beats' (as he tantalisingly abbreviates them to this day) were the best, he insisted; they had carved their sound from the American music they loved, popular music with soul, particularly that made by Ray Charles, Chuck Berry and the fast-emerging artists of the Tamla Motown label. Marsden was an engaging, cheery, energetic twenty-one-year-old and it would have been a sour man indeed who did not respond to his exuberance.

It would have been easy to mistake Gerry for a transient pop star unable to survive more than a few years. But he was deceptively serious about his work and as his career unfolded he became fiercely ambitious. The Liverpool grit that shaped him was to play a significant part in his longevity during the tough decades that followed his launch.

On stage, he's alive with *joie de vivre*. This is his natural milieu and he draws strength as he faces audiences from Chelmsford to Sydney, from New York to Liverpool. The effervescent songs communicate, but so also does his clear delight at being there, and his determination to send everyone home happily.

Off stage, he can be tough, abrasive, bossy and impatient, but always honest. With Gerry you know precisely where you stand within a minute of encountering him. A hard-headed businessman, he is also deeply sentimental.

The idea for this book began in 1990. Gerry and I were guest speakers at Beatlefest, the American fans' convention run by Mark Lapidos. I had attended many Beatlefests through the years, in New York, Chicago and Los Angeles, and had heard many guest speakers from the Beatles era. Gerry was, in my view, the most eloquent ever to appear. With his guitar by his side, he told fresh stories of the 1960s and beyond – many of them against himself – with candour and wonderful humour, and with a Liverpudlian ring of authority. When there was a natural break in his speech or between the questions from the audience, he would pick up his acoustic guitar and ad-lib a Beatles song, or one of his own, with an impromptu charm that capitivated the audiences.

Listening to his amusing, informative anecdotes on his Liverpool years alongside 'the Beats', Mark Lapidos and I were convinced he should write his autobiography to expand on those stories.

Gerry was uncharacteristically bashful at first, but after some persuasion, particularly from his manager Derek Franks, he tore into this project with his usual impulsive, compulsive enthusiasm. The result is, I hope, a breezy account of his extraordinary first fifty years.

Our thanks for help with preparing this book go to Pauline, Gerry's wife, to whom he has been happily married since 1965 ('but if you take away my absences while travelling or on the stage, it only adds up to a year and a half of marriage,' he says); to Derek Franks, Gerry's friend, manager and supporter; to Mitch Murray, Tony Barrow, Ron Richards, Ann Wilson, Bob Wooler, Derek Harknett, Danny Betesh and Pete Waterman. We are grateful to Phil Tucker, Gerry's British fan club president, for his unique help, particularly with the compilation of the discography of Gerry's record career which appears at the end of the book. I should like to thank my wife Pamela and sons Miles and Mark for their support. Gerry and I are grateful to David Reynolds and Penny Phillips at Bloomsbury Publishing, and Lavinia Trevor at the William Morris literary agency.

My thanks, above all, to Gerry, a valued friend who exudes the best in human values. After thirty years of creditable survival in the show-business jungle, he plays on because he truly loves spreading '60s smiles into the 1990s and beyond. He'll always be in orbit.

Ray Coleman
Spring 1993

1

On the Streets of Liverpool

Fighting Fit

It's not surprising that I now find it easy to live out of a suitcase when I'm travelling the world – I spent part of my life as a baby literally inside one! I was a war child and during the air-raids my mother put me in a suitcase under the stairs because she didn't like going down into the air-raid shelters. She even put my brother Fred under the stairs along with me; he was placed in a chest of drawers.

I was born Gerard, the second son of Mary and Frederick Marsden, on 24 September, 1942. I remember my mother telling me that bombs had flattened Miller Street, near where we lived in the Dingle, Liverpool. Our canary was killed by flying glass coming through the kitchen window. The war is a blurred memory as far as I'm concerned, but a left-over from those years became part of my growing up: I used those air-raid shelters as a kind of 'stage' on which to stand and sing. These were Gerry Marsden's first 'performances'.

My brother Fred, two years older than me, and I shared a happy childhood: we enjoyed doing all the things kids do, like looking for conkers on the trees. But as I grew up, the reality of life in the Dingle taught kids to look after themselves in every way. You learned to fight, or you'd get punched. Nearly all the streets had gangs. Mine was the Menzies Street Mob. There were about twenty-five gangs in the Toxteth area and we learned from a very young age not to stray into rival territories without expecting trouble.

Everybody guarded their own area. It was punching and kicking – 'Protect your nose, teeth and groin' we were told, for as far back into my childhood as I can remember. So fighting became part of my growing up.

I love boxers – in fact, all my family were boxers except my brother Fred, he was an Alsatian! I admire boxers largely because they represent courage. There's something special about sitting on a stool in the corner of the ring, looking at the guy opposite, and knowing he's out to beat you with his skill and nothing else. And I respect boxers for that. Once that bell rings, it's you and him; only the referee can interfere.

In a strange way you love this fighter for his guts and want to put him on the ground as quickly as possible with the least damage. You don't want to kill him, you just want to put him to sleep. Boxing is still in my blood, but these days I only punch a bag in my gym for fifteen minutes a day, and watch every fight I can on television.

It was my natural inclination to fight that led to my going into show business. Since the age of eleven, I'd been boxing at my school, Our Lady of Mount Carmel, and enjoying it. I was an eight-stone-six, five-feet-tall bantamweight, winning more than losing my fights, boxing for the school. And I decided to get more practice by boxing at the Florence Institute three nights a week.

I regularly fought Alan Rudkin at the Institute. Besides being a good mate, he was an excellent fighter. But one night, he wasn't messing. He laid into me really badly and when I got him in a clinch, I said, 'Alan, what *are* you doing?' It felt like some strange power had got into him.

He said, 'I dunno, but I feel tremendous.'

And I said, 'And I feel bleedin' awful, as if you're really battering me.'

Alan said, 'I can't help it. I feel great.'

I said, 'I'm glad *you* do, because I'm knackered.'

We broke from the clinch and he continued to knock absolute hell out of me. At the end of the fight I went home with my eyes, mouth and lips badly swollen. My mother looked at me in horror.

'What happened?' she asked.

'He battered me, and I'm never gonna box again,' I replied. My mother was amazed because she knew how much I loved boxing. I added, 'Alan Rudkin has just found out what he's got to do to become what he will be one day, a champion boxer.' She told me I was silly, but I said, 'Honest to God, I'll never box again. I'm staying with music.'

I put my boxing gloves in their box and never wore them again. At seventeen I went for music with tunnel vision. Four years later, we started scoring hit records – and Alan Rudkin was the British Commonwealth and European Bantam-weight champion, and a dear friend of mine for life. Alan, I can't thank you enough for finding that magnificent purity in your fighting – and for giving me such a hiding that night at the Florence Institute!

Music has been in my life since I was about four. It all began with my father's ukulele playing. Every Saturday night he and my mother would go to the pub near our house for a sing-song while my brother Fred and I sat on the front doorstep watching the world go by. I could hardly wait for them to return, because then my mother would make the sandwiches and their singing would continue. I'd join in. That's how I got my first musical ideas; and I remember standing on the air-raid shelter in Menzies Street when I was about five singing 'Ragtime Cowboy Joe'.

My parents were not well off, but they weren't skint either. They worked hard for everything. Dad was a railway clerk and my mother cleaned the school I attended and she also worked in the local fish and chip shop.

The house where I was born, at 8 Menzies Street, in the heart of Dingle, was a warm and cosy terraced house with parlour, kitchen and back scullery and two bedrooms. I shared one of these with my brother Fred, who is two years older than me. Life was tough, but we did not starve and we were raised in good values. We saved to buy everything – like the old big glass radio with the battery in the back. Dad made me a steering cart which passed for a bike.

Just after the war, everybody was watching money, but the atmosphere of Dingle was very neighbour-friendly as well as tough: we used to borrow sugar, milk, bread. I'd throw a piece of coal or a brick over the wall, hit the back door of our neighbour Alf Mandy, and shout: 'Alf – got some milk and sugar?' And he'd pass it over the wall. That was the kind of area it was: great fun, happy times, great people. Life was hard but there was a spirit.

There was a rag and bone shop in Mill Street where they gave us money for almost anything: we used to go around asking people for bits of leather, old shoes and old rags, or literally any rubbish, and take it down there for a halfpenny or even a farthing. The war had left a lot of derelict buildings and we used to take the lead and pipes off the roofs and sell 'em.

When I reached Our Lady of Mount Carmel school, I enjoyed all the lessons and wasn't at all bad academically. But music was special. Sometimes the teacher would ask me to take charge of the music class and my way of doing that was to show off by singing a song. It was called swanking. I was in the school choir and the church choir, and Dad saw the writing on the wall. Whenever there was pop music on the radio, my ears were glued to it.

We were always fighting. There was a scrap in the school playground every day. It amazes me when I meet people who tell me they've never had a fight in their lives. I can't comprehend that, because in the Dingle, we never had a day when we didn't. If a day passed when there wasn't a battle, we'd say, 'What *happened* today, then?'

I might have been a slight kid, but I always had a battling instinct and, in the spirit of Liverpool, I never took anything lying down, except when I made a bed in the woodwork class at school and tested it, because wood, then as now, was my favourite thing to work with as a hobby.

At that time of my life my father had a ukulele which he had managed to save and bring home from the ship in which he'd been torpedoed during the war. I played the uke all the time and he showed me a few chords. When my Uncle Peter died, my Auntie Lily asked me if I wanted to learn to play on his big old Spanish guitar, so I began trying myself on that. Then, when I was twelve, my dad arrived home one day with a big brown bag and said that inside it was a 'surprise' gift for me. It was my first guitar, a twenty-five pound Spanish acoustic with a cut-away so that you could get your hands further down the neck. I'd never seen anything like this. Woweeeeeeeeeee! I was 'made up!'

We couldn't afford lessons, so I transposed all my father's chords from the ukulele to the guitar, adding an extra two strings. Then I bought Bert Weedon's book, *Learn To Play In A Day*, which influenced many thousands of young kids like me. Later in my career, I had the opportunity to appear on the same stage as Bert Weedon and was able to tell him that his book had helped me to learn to play.

'God bless you, Gerry!' he said; he is still a dear friend.

Dingle was no place for strangers and even if you lived there, you kept strictly to your own area. There were dozens of gangs and we learned to take care of ourselves. There was hardly any reason for the fights – our Menzies Street Mob would meet another gang from another street and there'd be a few bloody noses or swollen mouths. We just accepted it as part of growing up, and it was a good 'laff'.

Luckily, these gangs called truces for certain things, such as delivering the papers. To earn money for records and guitar plectrums and strings, I delivered the Liverpool *Echo* every afternoon after school. It was important to get permission from rival gangs to go into their territory. Even if you'd had a punch-up a few days earlier, they'd let you in. If you were delivering the *Echo* through the letter-box for their dad, you were OK.

9

And this was vital to my musical education, because on Saturdays when I delivered the sports editions I'd run in and out of the houses and ask if I could watch just a snatch of two television shows famous in those years, 'Six Five Special' and 'Oh Boy!' It was great to catch the pop hits of the day in this way and I especially liked the skiffle stuff of Lonnie Donegan ('Rock Island Line', 'Cumberland Gap' and 'Alabammy Bound'), Chas McDevitt and Shirley Douglas ('Freight Train') and Johnny Duncan and his Bluegrass Boys ('Last Train To San Fernando').

At home, we were disciplined properly, never allowed to swear – if I said 'bloody' my mother would swipe me – and when I left school at fifteen I had to earn my own money. As a part-time job I worked heaving coal in the Dingle. Delivering one hundred-weight sacks up five flights of tenement stairs wasn't easy, but I didn't feel the weight so much because it was resting on my shoulders. I spent hours in that coal yard, even in the snow and rain, shovelling hundred-weights of coal for people who came with their bags. Jimmy Diamond, the man who owned the coal firm, would give me a pound for a day's work. It wasn't much, but it was money that I could save towards a new guitar or amplifier.

On leaving school, my first real job was at the Kardomah tea factory in central Liverpool, helping to make tea-chests. Even in this setting, there was music all around me: we all used to stand and sing the hit songs of the day while we made the chests. One lad was a great country and western fan and we had a great time singing those tunes. Making tea-chests for a living was really ironic in view of how, later, in my skiffle group, we'd put string on a broom handle, attach it to the tea chest, and use it as a double-bass.

I cycled to work. I wouldn't waste money on the bus. I can't remember a time during those years when I wasn't saving for something to do with my music – a new guitar, an amplifier, or a better model to improve the sound.

It was freezing in winter on that long ride to Red Cross Street near the docks, where I worked, but I didn't mind. I was young and had a bike, whereas thousands of others had to walk to work. The things that are taken for granted now as part of childhood were more special in those post-war days of the 1950s.

After a few months making tea-chests I wanted a change so I went to Woolworth's, brushing out and taking the ice-cream trolley round the store shouting 'Mind yer backs, please!' There were some strange looks from the customers at this madman rushing round the store like a lunatic at great speed.

Then my dad, who worked as a railway clerk, decided it was time I got a job with some kind of future, so he got me a position as a railway-van delivery boy. This was hard work because of the hours. Working most nights with my skiffle group, I didn't get home until about two o'clock in the morning, and I had to be on the wagon at the railway depot at six o'clock. I was so tired that the driver let me grab a sleep in the back of the van during deliveries! Then he'd shout, 'Get up!' and I'd have to shake myself up, and unload the fish I'd been sleeping next to. I stank to high heaven – and I've been a slippery customer ever since!

I worked from 6 a.m. until 6 p.m., unloading the fish train and delivering supplies around the markets. For this I earned seventeen pounds a week. It was horrendous. In summer the smell was a killer and in winter the work froze my bones. But I got to know every inch of Liverpool dockside with those deliveries.

It was the skiffle age. In 1956 Lonnie Donegan's 'Rock Island Line' had inspired everybody. My group consisted of my brother Fred, who cut the top out of a biscuit tin with a can opener, got some parchment paper and put it in, and jammed the top on; he bought some brushes and became the drummer. My Dingle pals Tommy Ryan and Dixie Dean joined us on washboard, Jimmy Tobin was on tea-chest bass and Matty Summers was the other guitarist. Brian O'Hara, who later helped form the Fourmost, also played guitar with us. Gerry Marsden's Skiffle Group, with my dad as manager, were 'available for engagements'. Dad arranged our first gig at the Peel Street Labour Party Club

11

in Dingle – for fourteen shillings and sixpence. We played a
lot at the nearby Florence Institute, the boys' club where I had
boxed, and even as a young group we played in front of the
Lord Mayor of Liverpool.

We went by bus, usually to youth clubs all round Liverpool.
Bob Wooler, later to become a major figure on the Liverpool
pop scene, recalls seeing me at the Peel Street Club in 1958.
He was the compère and stage manager for other venues, and
got me my first big show at Holyoake Hall, Huyton. We were
paid three pounds.

My dad helped us lug this great tea-chest and he seemed to
have an argument nearly every night with bus conductors who
didn't want it on board. There was very little money from the
skiffle group – we were lucky to get a few bob that paid the
bus fares – but we enjoyed it.

There were literally hundreds of groups like ours forming.
Over in Woolton, John Lennon had formed one called the
Quarry Men, but we didn't know that would develop into
anything special! Our groups played the same circuit.

The Quarry Men was originally John Lennon's skiffle group,
but I didn't see them until Paul McCartney joined them. They
weren't as good as my group, really. John and Paul stood out
as talented right from the start, but the rest of the sound was
rubbish.

John and I unknowingly shared the two inspirations that
marked our lives: Lonnie Donegan and Elvis Presley. It was
Presley's 'Heartbreak Hotel' and 'Hound Dog' that hit us both
in the gut with the new sound of 'rock 'n' roll'. I remember
often going to the house of a school friend, David Sefton, to
play records. His brother had just bought 'Heartbreak Hotel'
and when I heard it, I said to myself, 'Cor, that's good, and
it's *not skiffle!*'

It was a period of tremendous discovery for pop fans like
me. A whole load of names that would become legends were
just beginning – Fats Domino, Little Richard, Ray Charles and
Jerry Lee Lewis. When I heard Jerry Lee's piano on 'Whole

Lotta Shakin' Goin' On', and then the piano on Elvis's 'Don't Be Cruel', I knew I had to change the whole thinking of my group. I started looking around for a rocking pianist and found a mate up the road, Arthur McMahon, who was interested in joining. There were quite a few comings and goings in the group around this time, but the basic line-up was me, Jimmy Tobin (bass), brother Fred on drums and Dixie Dean (washboard).

Liverpool was becoming quite competitive, musically, and we did an audition for the major London figure-head of those years, Larry Parnes, who managed such prominent artists as Georgie Fame, Tommy Steele and Marty Wilde. Looking for an act to tour with one of his big names, a Liverpudlian singer named Billy Fury, Parnes conducted an audition on 10 May 1960 at the Wyvern Social Club in Seel Street, Liverpool, premises which Allan Williams, well known in the city as a rock 'n' roll entrepreneur, would later call the Blue Angel.

There was no piano available, so Arthur McMahon played guitar that day. Also on the audition was a band then called the Silver Beetles; they had a bass player named Stu Sutcliffe who did the entire audition with his back to Larry Parnes and Billy Fury, because he didn't want it to be seen that he couldn't play the bass properly! We didn't pass the audition, and though the Beatles did, Parnes said the bass player was useless and they should join the Fury tour without him. John Lennon said that if his mate Stu wasn't invited on the tour, they wouldn't go as a group. So they didn't do the Billy Fury tour either.

That was the only time Arthur McMahon played bass instead of piano for my group, and from then on, it was pure rock 'n' roll for me.

The piano gave us an edge over most other groups. Our sound was more accurate in recreating the American hit songs, whereas most of the others had to rely on playing the piano bits on their guitars.

All the musicians in Liverpool would hang out at Hessy's, the Whitechapel instrument shop just around the corner from Brian Epstein's record store. There was a guy in there who really knew about guitars, strings, plectrums, drumsticks, and he became 'Big Daddy' to us all. Before the Beatles arrived, the most prominent local musician was Jim Gretty. He played mouth organ and sang country and western music in a white cowboy suit with boots and a Stetson. Jim had no interest in rock 'n' roll, but he took all the groups under his wing with some excellent advice on what we needed – and he let us play around with the new guitars in the shop. It was like a wonderland to us and we'd all meet in there: 'Hi, Gerry, have you seen this new Fender and Gibson? Go on, you can have a go on it.' Heaven!

We met all the groups in Hessy's and swapped experiences as we tried out great guitars we couldn't afford, like Gretsch's. Colin Manley of the Remo Four, the best guitarist in Liverpool, was always in Hessy's and I used to sit watching his hands till he'd say, 'Clear off, you're not copying me, Marsden.' He still says it today, the swine!

With the money I'd been saving from work, I bought a huge Zenith acoustic which I'd play around the clubs and pubs like the Windsor Castle; but the first serious electric guitar I bought from Hessy's was a forty-pound Futurama, a model also favoured by George Harrison in those years. I glued coloured stones across the body – red, yellow, blue and white – so they shone magnificently as imitation diamonds. I felt like Jack the Lad.

Now a new name was needed, because we'd dropped skiffle.

We decided on Gerry and the Mars Bars – Mars from Marsden, Bars because it related to music. The speed of things was exciting around Liverpool. I was heading for show business as a career. I told the neighbours, and naturally they thought it was just a kid with high hopes. But looking back, it was always going to be entertainment for me: I liked to be involved in whatever I did. In football, I wanted to be the goalkeeper, in cricket the wicketkeeper, because I then felt at the centre of the game. I enjoyed swimming and diving, and still do today. When the church choir called for a soloist in 'Ave Maria', I volunteered to sing it. And one of the parents gave me a one-shilling piece which I kept for many years as a lucky mascot. This episode reminds me that in my infant school days, I was part of a choir which the headmaster, Mr Killakelly, formed. He called us the Luton Girls' Choir; only problem was, we were all boys. But anyway, back to the story . . .

The determination to be a leader might have been because I was pretty short, only five feet five and a half inches. Most of my mates were taller. That made me fight a bit harder, want to be the boss. In the pub, I always volunteered to lead the singing and at music lessons, it was the same. I loved to see people clapping, feeling happy. And I still do. Seeing pleasure on people's faces is life's blood to me. What I do now dates back to when I was a kid: I always wanted to have people laughing and smiling within two minutes of meeting them.

By 1958, when I was sixteen and on the railways, the music scene in Liverpool was throbbing with hundreds of rock 'n' roll groups, and I should think parents the length and breadth of Merseyside were warning their sons that they wouldn't be able to rely on 'this pop stuff' for a living.

My ambition for a career on the stage was pretty strong then. I went for an audition for a film role as an extra in a film called *Violent Playground*: they were looking for schoolkids, but rejected me because I was too short. The film was set in Liverpool and the star was someone who is now a good friend, Frankie Vaughan.

But luckily the music 'circuit' was growing to keep my interest up. Gradually, clubs that had always booked only traditional jazz bands realised that there was something almost unstoppable, because there were so many pop groups asking them for dates.

About this time my dad wrote to Mars, the chocolate people, and asked if they minded if we used their name. We needed to be sure of ourselves, wanted to feel it was official. But they replied that their name was strictly their copyright and therefore we had to drop 'Mars Bars'.

Their loss proved my gain. I was watching some athletics on television when the commentator referred to the 'pacemaker' for the race. I went to the band with the new name, 'Gerry and the Pacemakers'. I'd set a new line-up, trimmed it down to four. Fred, my brother, was by now a good drummer; we had Arthur at the piano, me on guitar and vocals; and Les Chadwick, whom we'd heard about in the famous Grapes pub in Mathew Street, Liverpool, joined us regularly on bass. We were getting quite a lot of work, still with my dad as the booker and manager, at places like Holyoake Hall in Penny Lane, Blair Hall, Aigburth Institute and the Iron Door. It was switching slowly from youth club centres to clubs and dance halls, but there was still a strong jazz 'thing' to overcome. Bands like Kenny Ball, the Saints from Manchester, the Merseysippi from Liverpool and Humphrey Lyttelton and Terry Lightfoot from London were to be seen advertised alongside new pop groups home-grown in Liverpool – King Size Taylor and the Dominoes, Johnny Sandon and the Remo Four, the Searchers, the Zodiacs, the Blue Genes (later the Swinging Blue Jeans) – and Gerry and the Pacemakers. And by then, Lennon's old Quarry Men had gone through several names to become, finally, the Beatles.

Some of our shows were promoted by Bob Wooler. He recalls that I scored one of my biggest impacts at a one-night stand at Liverpool Stadium on 3 May 1960. Bob tells me: 'I shall never forget Gerry singing "What In The World's Come Over You?", which went over really great with the audience.'

Bob also remembers the difficulty which we often had because of having a pianist. 'It was touch and go whether they appeared that night,' he remembers about one occasion, 'because Allan Williams [the promoter] failed to get a piano to set up in the boxing ring where the group played minus the ropes. I prevailed on them to do the show but Arthur McMahon was disgruntled at having to go on with a guitar.'

The standard of pianos at the venues was a recurring problem.

They were battered old things, out of tune and didn't do our sound any favours. But we felt we were distinctive.

I was friendly with all the groups. We'd bump into each other in a record store called NEMS in the centre of Liverpool. That's where I got to meet John Lennon and Paul McCartney. We were all doing the same thing: inquiring about the new rock 'n' roll hits from the States by people like Chuck Berry, Bo Diddley, Jerry Lee Lewis. We liked music that had balls, and a lot of it by black artists. All this puzzled the manager, a quietly spoken and well-dressed man named Brian Epstein, who was a bit older than us. He always seemed a little flummoxed by the artists' names we were mentioning to him. We liked him, though, and he was helpful, trying to get us the records.

At this stage Brian knew nothing about our shows, though only a couple of hundred yards from his office was the Cavern Club in Mathew Street. It was a stronghold of jazz bands, some of which came from London. This frustrated us. Paul McCartney and I often approached the club manager, Ray McFall, on behalf of our bands, asking for dates there – it would be good prestige to play right in the centre of town. But he refused us for what seemed like months. 'Can we work here?' we'd say when we wandered over there. 'No, it's a jazz club and we don't want rock 'n' roll, it's crap,' he'd say.

Well, we persisted. Finally, he agreed to try us out at lunchtime sessions, to catch the young workers who popped in for a soup, a cheese roll and a soft drink between noon and two o'clock. We alternated two or three days a week with the Beatles – and the results were amazing. The place was packed. My wife-to-be – whom I had not yet met – was among the office workers who would change from their working clothes into the fashionable duffle coat to come to the Cavern – and then go back to change again when they returned to their desks.

Bob Wooler was the resident compère at the Cavern. We shared the same employer – he worked as a railway clerk out at Garston – and Bob's knowledge of pop was a big influence on us and all the groups. He called me 'Mr Personality' and 'The

Grin Master' to acknowledge my smile, and he encouraged us. The song he used as his 'play out' signature tune, Bobby Darin's 'I'll Be There', became a favourite of mine and I recorded it once my career got moving.

According to Bob Wooler, I was 'very publicity conscious and would give the fans what they wanted. Everything was always in Gerry's smile. He had this natural way of presenting himself ... and he could charm.'

It wasn't long before Ray McFall realised there was a huge following for the pop groups and he put us and the Beatles on at nights. This was the start of the revolution! People then flocked to the Cavern, but they came for rock 'n' roll instead of jazz. I reckon Ray McFall should have paid Paul McCartney and me commission on all the extra money he made, because if it hadn't been for us pestering him, the Cavern would have remained a jazz club.

We were all teenagers while this was going on and I was still on the railways. Such was the energy around, though, that we played most nights. I became very friendly with the Beatles – Lennon, McCartney, George Harrison and their drummer Pete Best – but only off stage. On stage, I saw them as our biggest threat and I simply wanted to bury them musically. Sometimes, they'd follow us on stage at a concert or at the Cavern, and we'd vow to make them work harder.

Even in these stages, I saw that the front line of John and Paul was tremendously talented: the two of them contrasted with each other very well. The battle to be first to play a new American hit was real, particularly between the Pacemakers and them.

We had a professional bond, though. These were the days before we wrote our own material properly, or if we did we didn't have much confidence to play it. So we were doing 'cover' versions of American hits, in my case 'What'd I Say?', and 'Hallelujah I Love Her So' by Ray Charles, 'Things' by Bobby Darin, and a beautiful song which I'd picked out from a film – this was 'You'll Never Walk Alone' by Rodgers and

Hammerstein from *Carousel*. When John and Paul found a new song we liked, and we wanted to change our 'live' set, we'd trade with them: 'If you let me play your "Jambalaya", I'll give you my "Roll Over Beethoven".'

I developed a special affinity with John Lennon. We had similar outlooks and the same sick sense of humour. John had left Liverpool College of Art when he was seventeen and didn't seem to have much of a career beyond rock 'n' roll. He was brilliant and he had a sharp mind, and whatever he did with the Beatles, even as a guitarist, was just *different*. I thought even then that Lennon and McCartney were unstoppable, like an express train that had to roar out of Liverpool.

Considering my age and the fact that it was so far only a hobby that earned a few quid, I took my music very seriously. I never believed that rock 'n' rollers should look like a bunch of scruffs. To me, it was a branch of show business, and that meant dressing smartly. We wore either royal blue jackets with gold buttons and red handkerchiefs with our initials G. P. sewn on the top pocket by my mother, or jeans and a T-shirt. But it had to look smart. I used to joke that the initials stood for the 'Goose Pimples'.

At home, the terraced house we lived in was small, so the neighbours could easily hear me practising in the front parlour. I always recall telling my mum and dad, and our neighbours Mrs Manley and Mrs Taggart, 'One day when I'm famous, I'll let you come to my concerts.' They found it hard to believe, but they saw I was really determined. I kept on: 'I'm gonna be a singer, gonna be in show business.'

Liverpool had a variety of clubs; the Beatles and their crowd used to hang around at the Jacaranda in Seel Street, which was run by Allan Williams. I went there a few times, but it wasn't really my scene: it was a bit too arty for me. The arty types weren't my sort of people. John Lennon used to hang around with his flat-mate from art college, Stuart Sutcliffe, but though we spoke we didn't have much in common. John pulled him into the Beatles as bass player but he couldn't play, so he used to stand with his back to the audience. As I mentioned earlier, he did this so he didn't get found out. It was a matter of a mate joining the band.

One of the biggest turning points in my life came from Germany. News of the Liverpool beat groups, as we called ourselves, filtered across to Hamburg, where there were a lot of clubs. A promoter named Peter Eckhorn arrived in town, and met Allan Williams, who asked me if I wanted to go and play in Germany. What an amazing idea! The group and I had never played farther from home than Manchester and, apart from summer holidays every year at Thornton Cleveleys near Blackpool, I'd not been anywhere else.

We jumped at it. My parents were naturally concerned at the prospect of a teenage son going abroad. They were even more worried when I said I was packing in my job at the railways. 'Be careful,' my mum said. 'We won the war. Is it safe to go to Germany?' I told her it was a long time ago. 'Well,' she said, 'you never know with the Germans!' It was that post-war period of fear.

Next I went to see my railway boss, Mr Pope. He knew I was in a pop group at nights but he was amazed when I said I was leaving to be a full-time singer and guitarist. 'I hope you realise,' he told me, 'that if you stayed with us, then within three years you would be a *train washer*!!!' I said no, I was off. I'd been earning about seventeen pounds a week through a load of overtime. Some of the drivers I'd become mates with, like Dick Forrester, warned me that it was a hell of a dangerous step to take, chucking in steady pay for pop music. 'Don't worry,' I told them. 'When I make it as an entertainer, I'll come down and see you.'

I was eighteen. Within days we were on the train to Hamburg from Liverpool via Harwich and the Hook of Holland. It was really freezing when we arrived and we wore our big long railway coats and tough boots, and all four of us – my brother Fred, Arthur McMahon, Les Chadwick and me – looked like death. Our first contact was Peter Eckhorn.

'My God!' he said when he caught sight of us at the railway station. 'Are *you* Gerry and the Pacemakers?' We looked more like tramps. I assured him we'd been travelling for two days and we'd be ready for work, whenever that was. We were due to mark the opening of a club called the Top Ten which at the very moment we arrived was full of builders, as it was being converted from a circus called the Hippodrome. 'You're on *tonight* at seven o'clock,' Peter replied. I said the place would never be finished in time, but he was insistent that the club's opening was that evening.

He sent us to our crummy flat – basically four beds in a room above the club – and told us to be down and ready for 6.30 p.m.

We played that night, as every night for the rest of the two months we were there, from 7 p.m. until two o'clock next morning, with a fifteen-minute break every hour.

We'd been very hard on poor old Peter Eckhorn. Typical Scousers, not too keen to get on stage so soon after arriving, tired, hungry. 'Don't tell us *anything*,' we said. 'We won the war.' But we played that night after he'd sent us to our so-called flat with food.

After our show, Peter Eckhorn came to us and said, 'I can now tell you that this morning I died at the railway station. I think: what have I got, four little men who I bought for two months! But I hear you play and everybody says you are marvellous.'

Away from home, we became very good friends with Peter and men like Horst Fascher, who were the leading lights in the Hamburg club scene. Around the corner, at a club called the Kaiserkeller, the Beatles were playing.

Allan Williams had arranged for the Beatles to go to Hamburg and appear at the Kaiserkeller for a club owner named Bruno Koschmider, while we headed for the Top Ten. There was a Hamburg 'family' of club people and their names would pass into rock 'n' roll history for the chances they gave so many Liverpool bands.

The German audiences were fantastic. The kids danced, sang

and shouted and we soon worked out that they sent us free drinks for every request. That was a great incentive to learn what they wanted playing.

We were away for Christmas and New Year, and pretty lonely, but Hamburg was very formative for me. It saw the start of my life as a serious musician. It was gruelling, pushed our knowledge and our repertoire to the limit, but, young though we were, it changed us into hardened professionals. We'd sing everything we knew, night after night. The usual plan was to do an hour of songs of Elvis, an hour of Jerry Lee Lewis, an hour of Fats Domino. We were *so* short of material. It's amazing to reflect on how that fact alone helped our future career. We really didn't like the way we were repeating ourselves – strange though it sounds, for teenagers we were still pros in our little way – so to change things around for any of the songs, we'd do our own twelve-bar lead introduction to the rock 'n' roll classics.

We sang any words that came into our heads. 'The Germans won't understand anything, anyway,' we said. Then we said, well, hang on, why not write proper words to go with the little guitar runs that we were developing? So, as we had all day free, we began to write a few songs. Necessity, they say, is the mother of invention: that, basically, was the motivation.

I became very friendly with the Fascher family. I'd met Uwe Fascher in the Top Ten Club and found that the family had links with all the clubs on the Reeperbahn, some of them as bouncers in the strip clubs. Uwe told me his elder brother Horst was in jail and I went to visit him there, beginning a close friendship. With their other brother, Freddy, they became my 'family' in Hamburg. They were quite a crowd: Freddy absconded from a Borstal-like institution one night to come and see my show! I used to go to their home where their mother would cook meals for me; Mrs Fascher became my 'German mother'.

When Horst came out of prison, he got a job as a bouncer and then became part of the Star-Club with Manfred Weissleider. We started playing the Star-Club regularly and my friendship with Horst and his family continues to this day.

A great inspiration for a lot of us arriving in Germany was a guy named Tony Sheridan, a Cockney lad who had already been over there for a couple of years. He was a terrific singer and guitar player with a very strong sense of showmanship. We all learned a lot of guitar licks from Tony. I watched him carefully and learned a lot about singing and presentation. He had great voice control, was a bit of a madman off stage, and became part of the British gang. He was in and out of all the clubs on the Reeperbahn and showed all of us, including the Beatles, the ropes which he'd learned the hard way.

Though it was a matter of great pride not to play songs twice, the audiences often wanted us to repeat their favourites like 'Save The Last Dance For Me' or 'Will You Still Love Me Tomorrow?'. The fans were sending us free beers or Bacardi and Cokes up to the stage, so by two in the morning we were drunk and we'd play anything. But we had a kind of unwritten rule between us in which we didn't want anyone to say, 'Oh, you've played that before.' I think it was because it was such an exhausting schedule that we became determined to stand up to it.

Sometimes, when we finished at 2 a.m., we'd be relaxing with Horst Fascher and the club boss would leave a barman or waitress there and the drinks would start again. Someone would say, 'Have you heard this song?' and we'd put all our instruments back on, all the lights up, and jam among ourselves until five in the morning. Where we got the energy from was amazing. When you're eighteen or nineteen, you can handle it.

The days were spent sleeping. Then we'd walk (no taxi, because we were saving every penny) to the Seamen's Mission for dinner (we called it tea in those days). We had steak and beans and chips – every day! Then we'd go and do the show. In 1975, I went back to the Seamen's Mission to see everyone I'd not seen for years, and guess what we had to eat there? Steak and chips and beans!

On Sundays we'd go to the beach fifty miles away if the

weather was good. If it was cold, we'd stay in bed to keep warm because winters in Hamburg were bitter and there was nothing else to do that didn't cost Deutschmarks. One Christmas, Ringo and Rory Storm and others came round and we spent the holiday grumbling about how lonely and horrible we all felt. I remember Ringo falling down the stairs accidentally and ending up with his head in the toilet. We dragged him out and he was still singing!

Tony Sheridan's style extended beyond his music. He always looked good, too. He wore cowboy boots – they were just coming into style then and we all had to consider very carefully whether to spend thirteen pounds on a pair for ourselves. It was a load of money, but we were all heavily influenced by Tony. George Harrison bought a pair of leather pants for about eleven pounds and said he was frightened to tell his mother how much they cost.

Sheridan was such a strong entertainer that the Beatles sort of 'hi-jacked' him and he cut their first record with them in Hamburg for the bandleader Bert Kaempfert. They recorded a song called 'My Bonnie'. 'You swines!' I thought. They were one up on us in progress and I wanted to get even. George even tried to pull Tony into the Beatles permanently, saying, 'That'll be one in the eye for Gerry Marsden if we get back home with Tony Sheridan in our band.' Thank God Tony didn't join them, because they would then surely have buried us.

In Hamburg John Lennon and I spent a lot of time together, drinking and debauching ourselves. He was a really great mate to hang around with. One thing I loved about him was that you could have the most terrible arguments with him, want to kill him, and within ten minutes it would be forgotten. He never sulked or bore a grudge, with me anyway. When I argued with John, and I said, 'If you don't shut up I shall give you such a smack in the gob', we would be off for a drink within a minute.

There was a straight division between the people the Beatles and I mixed with in Hamburg. I veered towards the battlers, the rough and ready fighters. I felt very comfortable with these people: they spoke my language. The Beatles went for the arty clique.

There were a crowd of Germans who went down to the Kaiserkeller and became very close to John and Stuart Sutcliffe, his best friend. Astrid Kirchherr and her boyfriend at the time, Klaus Voormann, were among them; they came to see us at the Star-Club, too, but though we chatted and she was a lovely girl, there wasn't the same relationship that Astrid had with the Beatles. She was to be an important influence on them in their adoption of a certain style.

After one Hamburg trip, I remember the Beatles coming back to Liverpool in black leather and with new hair styles. Everybody laughed. 'Aaaaaaargh, what's this?' People said they hadn't bothered to comb their hair. It was a look which Astrid had created for them, and it was how they looked when they became famous as Beatles. She also influenced them to wear black leather. There was a very arty crowd in Hamburg – not for me, but it suited the lads.

I used to meet the Beatles separately from our chosen 'gangs'. They didn't mix with mine, the Faschers and their mates, and I didn't mix with theirs; we'd go out together for dinner, have a laugh, go to clubs where John and I would get drunk and shout too much. Then we'd go back to our own 'corners'.

I love John's voice, his distinctiveness as a singer and also as a guitarist. The way he played was instantly recognisable to me, totally different from the rest of us. He seemed to have absorbed all the rock 'n' roll influences and then come out the other side with entirely his own stamp as a musician. That's a great artist. Strangely, even as a young man, I used to think John looked rather like a Red Indian, whereas I look like a rabbi!

Because John was so individualistic, I wasn't so envious of John as I was of Paul. His voice, so soft and velvety, knocked me out. I've always found it hard to sing gently, and even on the ballads I have a bit of an edge. So Paul's singing was what

I really worried about. To myself, I'd often say, 'You bastard, Macca, you've got it, a natural voice.'

The needle, the hassle, between us was essential for kids of that age. The Beatles kept winning the readers' poll in *Mersey Beat* newspaper and, as McCartney said, that depended on who got up first in the morning to buy enough papers to distribute to their fans. The following year we won, as I got to the paper shop first.

We spent a lot of time in company with the Beatles but the rivalry was real enough. We'd drink with each other, but I always kept an eye on what they were doing on stage. It was like the boxer's mentality which has always been part of me: I'll have a drink with anyone and enjoy the chat, but once on stage, I'd want to win. We constantly tried to discover better songs than them. We respected each other's songs, but when the Beatles released the record 'Twist and Shout', which went on to become one of their favourites, a lot of Scousers were angry. They reckoned John and Paul had nicked it from King Size Taylor, who had found it from the original Isley Brothers version.

Rory Storm was the only real showman in Liverpool at that time, and I always regretted that he never made it properly. He was a natural-born entertainer and looked a million dollars on stage. Trouble was, he didn't have any male fans – only girls. The Beatles and I had loads of fellows liking our music as well as girls, so poor Rory was restricted.

King Size Taylor should have made it, too. He was a huge guy who dominated a stage, singing stuff like 'She's So Respectable' which I wanted to pinch but couldn't because he'd grabbed it. Great act. The Remo Four were another good band. Liverpool was teeming with 'em. Johnny Sandon sang with the Remos, and he was good.

One of the most memorable meetings in those Hamburg days was with Little Richard. We were appearing at the Star-Club and were in awe of meeting a real American star whose music we'd been studying and playing for years.

'Richard, it's such a pleasure to see you live; we've listened to your records for years,' we said.

'Oh, that's cool,' he said in that rather feminine, high-pitched voice of his. 'What are you guys called?' I told him and he sat watching us; we played at our best, as this was like an audition before God. As we came off, Richard said to us, 'Jeez, that was good. One day you're gonna be a star – but today you're just a little light bulb.' We'd made no records and he was just about right, as well as funny.

Four years later, he came to one of our shows in the States – by then, we'd had some success. 'My little light bulb has turned into a star!' he said to me. What a lovely man; and what an inspiration to all of us who were touched by rock 'n' roll in those years.

Fats Domino was another friend I made in the Star-Club. I sat watching his show in amazement night after night. 'God, that's amazing,' I would say as he came off the stage after his finale, 'When The Saints Go Marching In'. As he did this, *every night* a fight began between his saxophone player and his trombonist. I was worried.

'What's going on?' I asked Fats.

He replied, 'Oh, they've been with me for twenty years . . . and they fight every night. He either stands on his foot, or the trombonist knocks the saxophone out of his mouth, or they hit each other with instruments. If they don't fight one night, I get very worried and think there's something wrong!'

Back in Liverpool after that first visit to Hamburg, me mam said, 'Well, are you going back to work?' I replied that I was definitely going to be a full-time musician. We'd been treated wonderfully in Germany, I said, to her amazement. Dad was great.

'You always worked hard; go for it!' he told me.

It was a risk, but I was super-confident. At this point I got the line-up of Pacemakers who would shape my career. Arthur

McMahon left to get engaged and Les Maguire joined as our pianist. The Pacemakers had day jobs – Les Chadwick in the bank, Fred at a candlemaker's, and Les Maguire at a joiner's. I took the view that I was the only one who wasn't *losing* a great career if nothing happened. Me mam never moaned but she was worried about whether I could get enough work.

We advertised for engagements in the Liverpool *Echo*, bought a Morris estate car and then a Commer van, and began getting bookings as far afield as Shrewsbury and Manchester! There wasn't much money in it: you could book us for fifteen pounds. We were playing for love as much as money, it seemed. But things were about to happen to make Liverpool beat groups like mine, and our city itself, the talk of the country.

2

The Hits Begin

Liverpool Explodes

In the autumn of 1961, competition among the bands was rife. Bob Wooler, writing in the Liverpool pop paper *Mersey Beat*, put us second behind the Beatles in his important list of the Top Ten most popular groups. Rory Storm and the Hurricanes were third.

I had no quarrel with this. John and Paul were massively talented and whatever happened with the Beatles, I knew they would be big names eventually. I was at least as ambitious as them, though, and Hamburg had improved our show incredibly. Everybody talked about how tight we'd become as a band.

We returned to Hamburg about half a dozen times, to the Star-Club, where the Beatles had by then also played frequently. It was that experience that truly made Liverpool groups like ours hardened professionals. We learned how to deal with audiences, how to sing our voices out so they toughened like leather, how to cope with working almost round the clock, and how to gel truly as a unit.

People often ask what made Liverpool bands different, why there was such an explosion of talent in the city in the late 1950s. A lot of it was the determination to seek happiness among kids of my age, and John Lennon and Paul McCartney's age. When the war ended in 1945, I was three, John was five, Paul was three. By the time we were teenagers, when we all wanted a carefree good time, ships were coming into the docks and sailors into the pubs, and the atmosphere in Liverpool was unique in its spirit.

The groups were all forming when we got lucky and the Hamburg guys arrived saying to Allan Williams: 'All these bands, do they want to go to Germany?' *That's* what gave us something totally different from southern groups. We went there and worked ourselves stupid. And by the time we returned, we had this incredible rock 'n' roll edge, American songs being sung with a Scouse accent.

Living away from home for months on end, so young, short of money, gave us an attitude which no bands anywhere else in Britain experienced. Liverpool bands were really lucky to have the Hamburg link which never happened for those from Manchester (like the Hollies), Birmingham (like the Moody Blues) and London (like Brian Poole and the Tremeloes), however good they were. The Hamburg Experience made us unique.

Just as we had to watch our step as kids in the Dingle, we became conscious of territories with the band. We played certain places where anybody from the Dingle wasn't welcome. For eighteen months every Friday, we played an especially hostile club, Blair Hall in Walton Road. That area was definitely 'no go' for people from the Dingle. During that period, we had five or six fights, but the music won us through. They liked the band, so the scraps stopped.

Another problem area for Dingle-ites was Old Swan. Sometimes there'd be a fight there immediately after we finished playing. I recall one night when there was a horrendous fight while we were on stage – we were knocking them off as they came up for us – and I locked Pauline, then my girlfriend, and her friend in a dressing room by the side of the stage to protect them. Garston was another difficult place for lads from the Dingle. I got smacked about a few times; the lads in the band had a few knuckles gone, loose teeth, black eyes, the occasional kick in the privates if they were unlucky. But there were no legs broken; it was simply a question of guarding your patch and as Dingle lads visiting some of these places, we hoped we'd be able to get on stage in one piece, because we knew the music would convert everybody.

It was nothing to do with girls. If a Dingle-ite chatted your girl up within the Dingle, you'd give him a pasting, pure and simple. But in the ballrooms elsewhere the girls caused no problems at all. Normally, the girls would stand on one side of the ballroom, the lads on the other and they'd meet to dance and mostly separate after the dance. So there was never trouble on the lines of 'My girl fancies you', because the chaps didn't have one girl. It was gangs of lads out for a fight over territory. Don't cross the line, or you'll get smacked. We just got used to it, and always went to gigs prepared to defend ourselves.

'Gerry was most territorial in those days,' remembers Bob Wooler. 'When I booked him at Hambledon Hall in Huyton, about six miles from his home area, he'd say to me: "Oh, that's a dangerous area for us. We'll get some of the lads [from the Dingle] to come with us!" This was the seedy side of rock 'n' roll. People say it must have been fantastic in those days but I say they should take off their rose-coloured glasses.' Bob, who should know, recalls that Holyoake Hall and Blair Hall were particularly strong areas for my popularity, and that generally I wasn't the victim of the crowds shouting 'Get him off.' This isn't such a small point as it seems. Bob remembers that some bands, including Rory Storm because he showed off too much for some of the crowds, were booed and dragged off stage. He also notes that I appealed equally to both sexes, as the Beatles did.

The catapult our Liverpool scene needed happened unexpectedly. Back from Hamburg, the Beatles and our group would often pop into Brian Epstein's record store in Whitechapel. He asked me several times why I was inquiring about obscure records by names he'd never heard of, like Fats Domino and Arthur Alexander, and I said that with a busy band playing the clubs of Merseyside and Germany, I was always seeking new material. And the best, I said, was American.

Brian Epstein was a nice guy to chat to, but not 'one of us'. He wasn't into our music at all, but he was very proud of his record stock. In November 1961, after hearing about the scene at the Cavern, Brian saw the Beatles and signed them to management shortly afterwards.

I wasn't surprised. They had nothing to lose. We all liked Brian and at that stage of our lives recording careers were just a pipe dream.

I was in and out of Hamburg and travelling all over the North, while Brian Epstein was starting his six-month long haul of getting the Beatles a record deal. Then one night he came to the Cavern when we were playing and saw me after the show. He asked me if I wanted him to manage us. I was off to Hamburg again in a day or two and I said we could chat on my return.

A few months passed. Brian was extremely busy, travelling to and from London where he was rejected half a dozen times in his efforts to get the Beatles a record contract. My mind was on our busy schedule. By May 1962, though, Brian invited me to his office and said we should decide. He seemed confident he could do good things for me, but it wasn't the big deal it seems now. I said OK. My dad was handling the diary and the bookings, I told him. I added that I was fed up with being a skint rock 'n' roller and if he could improve our money, that would be great. He said he had no doubt about doing that.

We didn't anticipate making records at this stage. I gave him our diary and thought no more about it. He was just this nice posh guy who spoke proper English, not Scouse like me, dressed immaculately and ran a record shop owned by his father. I thought he could also get us some records cheap! I was very unconcerned with the seriousness of having a manager. So I signed as Brian's second act. His commission would be on a sliding scale to a maximum of twenty-five per cent of our fees.

Yet within a month of his signing us, two things had happened. Brian had increased our booking fee from fifteen to twenty pounds per night. And after a lot of heartache, he'd got the Beatles a recording contract with George Martin, the EMI Records producer. It was great for them and for Liverpool – and also for us, because Brian was telling everyone, 'The Beatles are going to make a record, and Gerry, my second signing, will be next.'

Remembering how he used to keep all the bands on their toes at the Cavern, Bob Wooler talks about his 'pained expression' and how he'd ask simply, 'Is that professional?' at some of our antics. But as Bob says, once Brian appeared on the scene and we headed for a recording career, we realised this was a different business and tightened our show considerably.

Brian was a positive influence on us. Being well groomed himself, he insisted that we smarten ourselves even more on stage. He caught us here and there wearing jeans, and even though they were smart, he said they'd have to go. Suits were needed for the stage. And if I did have to smoke, they should not be Woodbines but filter tips! Everything had to have *style* for Brian. I felt he was constructive in everything he said about our work, and I gave him more attention than I gave to others.

Rory Storm was a tremendous showman – better on stage, more natural, in fact, than either the Beatles or me. He dressed the part and acted the part. He was in show business as much as rock 'n' roll. It was sheer irony that while Rory was not destined to make it as a national star, he was to provide the Beatles with the drummer who helped them to shape their act. The issue of the Beatles' drummer was one of the most controversial things to happen in those early years in Liverpool

I'd known Pete Best quite well. As the Beatles' drummer, he seemed solid enough when I heard him in Hamburg and around town. What he played seemed right for their sound. But shortly after Brian signed me, hell broke loose. The Beatles and Brian decided to fire him, with no serious reason given. There were ructions among the fans.

Ringo was a natural choice of successor. Inside Rory Storm's band he had a star quality and charisma that stood out. He had a streak of grey in the middle of his hair which I think he'd painted in and he looked like someone special. I couldn't see him in any other band, like mine or the Remo Four or the Swinging Blue Jeans. It had to be the Beatles.

Musically, perhaps Ringo was slightly better than Pete Best. But the change wasn't necessary for that reason, in my opinion. I was pretty sure it was a political firing, which sprang from Pete being too handsome. He certainly attracted the girls and I think Brian saw his good looks as some kind of threat to Paul and John and George as they were just beginning the climb to national fame. Hence, they got Ringo!!! Whatever they planned for the Beatles, Pete clearly didn't figure in it, which was a tragedy of a kind. They asked my brother Fred to play with them, go to Hamburg with them, but he told them he had decided to stay with me, the biggest mistake he'd made in his life!

Everybody felt, as I did, that sacking Pete was a shabby thing to do. Shabbiness wasn't normally in Brian Epstein's repertoire, but this was just that.

'I don't care what you say in reply,' I told him. 'It's not my band, and nothing really to do with me, but I think you shit on Pete Best.'

'Oh, you don't understand,' Brian started to say.

'I'm not interested in who understands what,' I said. 'The way you've done it is wrong and nothing will ever change that. And people won't forget.'

Brian in his charming manner hummed and aaaaaaarghed and got on to a different subject.

Pete was really treated badly and he was sick that he'd been kicked out in the way he was.

'Gerry, what have I done?' he said to me.

I said, 'Peter, I don't know.'

The fans were really furious and with good reason. There were very ugly scenes and nobody was surprised about that. Brian Epstein got punched and I think he cried for about four days. Somebody wanted to smack Ringo, too. It was a massive

34

issue in Liverpool, like World War Three among the bands who felt strongly that Pete Best had been wronged when he was so popular.

I thought it was a tacky thing to do for no apparent reason. I was very annoyed also that when I'd asked Brian Epstein for a reason, he couldn't give me a proper answer. I thought it was a sour way to start a recording career for the Beatles, firing a drummer who'd been with them for two years. I told Pete Best – who wasn't particularly a mate of mine, but was an honest fella who got a bad deal – what I thought, but by then it was too late. The deed had been done. Ringo proved perfect, but the principle of Best's sacking left a nasty taste in the mouth as the Beatles began their climb out of Liverpool to the world stage.

On 5 October 1962, the Beatles released their début single, 'Love Me Do'. That was a colossal thing for Liverpool. They'd *been to London* and *made a record*. They'd cracked it! Looking back now, of course, it was just the tip of what we know happened later, but you had to be around as I was, a working musician, to know the importance of that record to all of us.

The world is inclined to think the whole Liverpool pop scene began with 'Love Me Do'. In fact, Epstein was fairly late in discovering all of us. There had been a lot of activity before Brian's arrival. At the start of the 1960s there were at least 250 pop groups in Liverpool, and the whole of Merseyside was brimming over with clubs and promoters. There was never any shortage of work: we could play every single night of the week if we wanted to, at such places as the Majestic, Birkenhead, the Orrell Park Ballroom, New Brighton Tower, Aintree Institute, the Cavern, Wilson Hall, Garston, the Iron Door.

We were so hungry for work that we played for peanuts. We laid ourselves wide open to being ripped off horrendously. The promoters were making a fortune. We'd ring them up and ask for a gig and they'd beat us down in price by saying, 'We don't know if you've got enough fans . . .' and then they'd knock us to stupid money, fifteen, ten or even five pounds a night.

Before Brian came along we earned twelve or fifteen pounds per show. That's what we'd get for promotions by guys like Sam Leach and Bob Wooler. It doesn't sound a fortune now but it wasn't bad money – when we could persuade certain promoters to part with it. It was often a battle to get the cash from some of them. We could get new equipment with it, save to buy a van and stage clothes.

Bob Wooler says:

Gerry had a far-reaching vision when success first came his way through Brian Epstein. Gerry did not lose his grip of the situation. It didn't go to his head in that way. He was a shrewd person and he has handled his money very skilfully. In Liverpool, he's always been regarded as a working-class lad (unlike John Lennon who came from a more comfortable background and area of the city). Gerry did extremely well for himself and good luck to him – that's most people's sentiment.

We didn't mind too much about the low rates of pay. We were learning, and by then I knew I wanted it to be my career. The huge difference came with Brian Epstein. He came in with his cool authority, told the Beatles and me, 'We'll raise the money or you don't play.' We were quite worried. I told him there were a million bands in Liverpool. 'Yes,' he said, 'but none as good as you and the Beatles.' Brian might have been stupid about money later, but in these early days he gave us and the Beatles a great belief in ourselves.

Brian went to all the promoters who'd been ripping us off for years and said, 'I'm looking after Gerry and the Beatles and from now on you will have to pay more money for their appearances.' Our rates went up overnight to twenty pounds and sometimes twenty-five. God bless him, he was great and had such style, but Brian was also naive. He signed contracts which in some cases tied us to places for nine months in advance – so that by the time we had hit records, we still had to play these places for twenty-five pounds. But Brian did have a vision for all of us; before he came on the scene, we'd only played outside Liverpool a few times, notably at a Manchester club called the Oasis. Brian got us work as far afield as Birmingham.

The Beatles' record 'Love Me Do' edged into the chart at number seventeen, which was low, but I knew they had a lot more to come and were on their way.

I was in Hamburg during a lot of the excitement that Brian and the Beats were having, and a letter I wrote to *Mersey Beat* at that time gives a flavour of what was happening to me:

We've been having a few experiences while we've been at the Star-Club. Fats Domino played here and brought the house down. After the show, Freddy [Marsden] and myself played with him for one and a half hours – it was really a swinging affair. His manager said that we were one of the best small combo's he's seen, so we were all very pleased.

Pat Boone was in the club for one night and I was talking to him. He was a very nice fellow. Unfortunately he couldn't sing due to a clause in his contract.

Little Richard has been here for a week and it's really been a great pleasure playing with such a good showman.

We would like to wish the Beatles (John, George, Paul and Ringo) all the best and congratulate them on the success of their first record, 'Love Me Do'.

Gerry and the Pacemakers
Star-Club, Grosse-Freiheit 39
St Pauli, Hamburg

While I was in Hamburg, I got a surprise phone call from Brian Epstein. He said the Beatles had turned down the offer of a song for their second single. They wanted to write their own.

Brian added that the unwanted song was called 'How Do You Do It?'. 'I'll send you over the demo record,' Brian said, 'and if you like it, learn it and I'll get George Martin to come and hear you because he's keen on the Beatles and hearing about other groups in Liverpool.'

By early December 1962 I was back in England and working the clubs as usual. George Martin came up to see the Beatles; originally, I didn't have a gig that night, but Brian had skilfully got us one at the Majestic, Birkenhead, at short notice, so that he could 'casually' invite George Martin to pop across and see us while he was in town. We'd learned 'How Do You Do It?' by then; I was told by Brian that Lennon had turned it down in favour of something he'd written called 'Please Please Me', which he hoped would be the next Beatles single. Adam Faith had also turned down 'How Do You Do It?', I was told. Well, all this didn't sit very comfortably with me, as it was a bit of a reject! But I had my eye firmly fixed on getting a foot into the record business, so my normal reaction was curbed a little by my determination to 'make it'.

My route to that first hit to launch my career properly was complicated – and the Beatles were heavily involved. In piecing together the origins of 'How Do You Do It?', I've had the help of Mitch Murray, who wrote the song, and Ron Richards, who was assistant to George Martin and whom George had put in charge of my recording sessions.

In those years, artists were generally not writing their own material. We relied on professionals who came through the songwriters' 'workshop' of Tin Pan Alley, which was, as far as we were concerned, Denmark Street in London. Mitch Murray had written about a dozen songs, nothing notable, and was desperate to get a hit. He recorded a demonstration lacquered acetate of his composition 'How Do You Do It?' and through his friend Barry Mason (later to co-write Tom Jones and Engelbert Humperdinck hits), he got his song to Ron Richards.

Mitch had written 'How Do You Do It?' with Adam Faith in mind. This was a few months before the Beatles and I had appeared on the scene. Ron Richards recalls:

I liked the song, but I had no use for it, so I put the demo record in my drawer . . . When George signed the Beatles he said to me, 'Have you got any songs?' I told him of 'How Do You Do It?' and he said, 'I quite like that, I'll send it off to them.'

Ron had also passed the word about the song to Dick James, a prominent London music publisher who would later figure largely in the careers of the Beatles, me and other Brian Epstein acts. Mitch Murray had not assigned the song to a publisher, and Ron knew Dick well.

Mitch Murray tells his side of it:

Dick called me to say there was this group from Liverpool called the Beatles which EMI Records was very excited about. They wanted the song to go to them. I said I was not very keen on that. I replied, 'This is a hit song and I don't want to give it away to some unknown bloody group.' But Dick convinced me to let them have a shot at it. He said to me, 'You haven't signed the publishing contract. If you don't like what they do, don't sign it.' He couldn't have been fairer.

'How Do You Do It?' was the first song the Beatles recorded for EMI. But, luckily for me, Mitch didn't approve of their version. He says now:

I thought the Beatles' version was bloody horrible, useless. They tried to harmonise with it and it's not a harmonic song. Their middle-eight treatment, with the oo-la-la, was awful. I thought this was a deliberate cock-up by the Beatles so they could get their own song through. I believed they'd screwed it up in the studio so their songs would have a better chance of being used. And of course, later, they admitted that was what had happened.

Dick James supported Mitch's views and told George Martin

that Mitch would not sign the publishing contract for the Beatles. Mitch remembers being present when Dick said to George, 'We've heard the record and we both agree that you've made an excellent demo!' It was a horrible thing to say, but he got away with it because George and he were very close. Mitch also wrote to George saying, 'Please don't issue this. They've ruined my song!'

I asked to hear the Beatles' version of the song and it was obvious they didn't want to do it. John was in a send-up mood; in the middle he sang in Buddy Holly style: 'Won't you tell me, h-h-how d-you do it.' He was obviously messing about.

After seeing us at the Majestic, George Martin told Brian that we didn't even need a record test; we should go to London and record the song. In January 1963, our van broke down on the journey south. It was snowing and freezing – and when George saw us it was like Peter Eckhorn's experience on our first Hamburg trip. We were full of grease from patching up the van and he sent us to our hotel to get some kip. I thought we'd blown it, because we felt we should have been on our best behaviour.

But everything went as smoothly as clockwork. When we'd finished recording it in an hour or so, George asked, 'Have you got a B-side which you've written?' I told him we had forty-seven billion songs of our own, and suggested 'Away From You', which I'd written with Les Chadwick. He liked it and we recorded it very quickly. Brian said we would sign to George for about five years. We didn't care about all that; we simply wanted a record out so we could show our kids something from our music days some time in the future when we were back on the railways or in other jobs!

Ron Richards was great to work with. He remembers how the Pacemakers and I arrived to record the song at 2.30 in the afternoon and finished it, together with the B-side, by 5.30. Ron was a real fan of the American pianist Floyd Cramer and encouraged Les to play the little solo on 'How Do You Do It?' that gives the song a kind of trademark.

Neither Ron nor others in the studio were sure about the song being successful but Dick James, who had a good ear for songs, was certain.

'Do you know,' he said to Ron, 'I think we've got a hit here.'

It was nice that the writer of the song approved our version and didn't like the Beatles'.

'Gerry's treatment was fantastic from the start,' Mitch Murray says. 'He outclassed our demo in every way!'

The greatest experience was hearing ourselves on a playback on tape in Abbey Road recording studios. It was like a dream, and when George said it was OK for release, we were over the moon.

I'd never heard a recording of the band and me – we'd messed around with tape recorders, but this was very different. My excitement was such that I said to George, 'Bloody hell, is that us?'

He said, 'I think that could be a hit', and Les Chadwick, Les Maguire and Fred and I all burst into laughter.

'Ah, don't be soft,' I said.

George was pretty serious about it. 'Well, you never know,' he said. 'It sounds nice. There's something nice and chirpy in the voice.'

George Martin was lovely. He knew we were only daft young kids doing our own thing. He gave us a lot of freedom without any lectures. We were a bunch of nutters who must have made quite a contrast for George from his regular artists like Matt Monro. His mixing engineer, Norman Smith, was shocked that these Scousers invaded their recording studio, bringing rum and Coke and swearing and smoking, putting their feet up on the mixing console. But George was gentle and put up with all that.

The Beatles went to the top of the *New Musical Express* chart on 22 February 1963 with 'Please Please Me', sharing the position with Frank Ifield's 'The Wayward Wind'. Meanwhile, we started getting reviews for 'How Do You Do It?'. In *Disc*, my voice was described as 'high pitched and biting . . . he strains a wee bit for effect . . . straight in the footsteps of the Beatles, this group has ideas and they deserve success.'

Elsewhere, Tony Barrow, who would later be our press officer, wrote about our 'cheerful, fast-moving number with an invigorating vocal. Gerry doesn't just sing his lyrics. He handles the slightly off-beat romantic theme with a plaintive vigour. Full-strength, hard-sell instrumental tactics from the Pacemakers as they pound out the hefty, rhythmic backing. Sizzling piano phrases by Les Maguire.'

On 1 March 1963 the single was released on EMI's Columbia label. Brian Epstein phoned me two weeks later, on Tuesday 19 March, to give me the greatest shock of my career at that stage. 'It's gone straight into the charts at seventeen, Gerry.' I thought he was kidding. We had just begun touring the country in a package tour Brian was promoting called 'Mersey Beat Showcase', leaving Liverpool in two coaches and going to cities to appear on the same bill as his growing stable of artists, the Beatles, Billy J. Kramer with the Dakotas, and the Big Three.

The records in the chart at that time show what a golden age we were experiencing in pop. The sounds and the names are still respected and enjoyed thirty years later: Jerry Lee Lewis was there with 'Good Golly, Miss Molly', Buddy Holly with 'Brown Eyed Handsome Man', Cliff Richard with 'Summer Holiday', the Shadows with 'Foot Tapper', Bobby Vee with 'The Night has a Thousand Eyes', Jet Harris and Tony Meehan with 'Diamonds', the Cascades with 'Rhythm of the Rain', Elvis Presley with 'One Broken Heart for Sale', Roy Orbison with 'In Dreams'. It was a tremendously exciting time. We were on great TV shows like 'Thank Your Lucky Stars' and 'Juke Box Jury' and we learned the importance of promotion. Brian had arranged for us to sign our music publishing interests with Dick James, who taught me a lot about how a record has to be launched, and also the value of writing the 'B' side to a hit single. You got just as much money from music publishing as if you'd written the 'A' side. The machinery of the music business began to interest me and Dick was an experienced and gifted teacher.

'How Do You Do It?' went from seventeen to five and then to the top on 3 April 1963. To follow the Beatles so quickly, and to do this with our first record, was sensational.

As soon as I heard the record had gone to number one, I rang Lennon: 'Hey, John, d'you remember that record that you didn't release and we did? "How Do You Do It?" – well, it's gone to number one.' He said, 'Shit', and a few other more unrepeatable words. But he was happy we'd got to the top.

Mars, the chocolate people, said we could now call ourselves the Mars Bars! Too late!

When I went home and announced the news, me mam said, 'What does that mean?' I said it meant I was suddenly famous, known nationally as well as in Liverpool. She said, 'You mean that after all these years of seeing Cliff Richard's name at the top, *you're* up there?' I said, 'Yeah, but it's only a great start. Look, Mum, I'm not going to leave this alone. I mean it now. I'm here to stay and I'm going to prove I can make it in show business.'

As soon as 'How Do You Do It?' entered the chart, Mitch Murray began work on a follow-up. It turned out that John Lennon, by then pretty ambitious as a songwriter, was hoping to be the writer of my second single. Up at Dick James' office one day, Lennon said to Murray, 'If you get that follow-up for Gerry with your song, I'll f—— thump you.'

Mitch replied, 'Listen, it will be worth a thump if I get that. I'll be happy.'

What happened was that Mitch wrote a song called 'I Like It' – which I did, immediately I heard it – and John's song was something called 'Hello, Little Girl', which became a hit for another Liverpool-Epstein group, the Fourmost.

Brian had lifted our money by about five pounds a night, but we had quite a few months of work at 'old money' to honour when he arrived. Even when we had a hit with 'How Do You Do It?', we had to play the Cavern cheaply because we'd signed the contract to appear six weeks before we'd hit the chart!

The Cavern has gone down in history as a kind of mystical place – but that's mainly because it's where Brian Epstein first saw the Beatles and Gerry and the Pacemakers. Apart from the great fans we developed down in that basement, it wasn't our favourite venue. It was a nightmare to get in and out of; struggling down the stairs from Mathew Street to the cellar with all our gear was tough, but it was the only entrance because there was no backstage – and no backstage toilet, either. I shudder to think of the effect of a fire down there, had there ever been one.

The Cavern had an atmosphere, right enough, for the fans. It stank of disinfectant and stale onions. It was hot, sweaty and oppressive. Blair Hall was ten times better, Holyoake Hall in Penny Lane was brilliant with a beautiful big stage and a dance floor the kids could enjoy. All the bands preferred it to the Cavern. If Brian Epstein had gone to any of these places to discover us and the Beatles, these venues would have been famous. But the Cavern went down in history.

With all the dates we honoured, not one of the promoters said, 'We're going to give you a few more pounds because now you have a hit, the place will be packed.' Brian said to us, 'You will never have to work for them again.' And we didn't.

We were proud of what we were achieving for the city of our birth. Years before we had broken through to national success, both the Beatles and my band had joined together for a memorable night of music at Litherland Town Hall. The joint 'band' was called the Beatmakers for this occasion, and looking back, it was probably the first big British rock 'n' roll 'event'. We had a great night, ending with John Lennon sitting underneath the piano and a few other crazy scenes, and we had a ball of a time.

Brian Epstein must have 'paired' me with John Lennon in his mind, for in the spring of 1963, he organised a joint interview by us in a London hotel for a British music paper.

'We're here,' John told the reporter, 'to promote the interests of over a hundred groups like ours.'

I interjected, 'Yours! Ours is different!'

John declared, 'There are about twenty top beat groups on Merseyside and several others who are not so big [he was only about three hundred short of the true figure]. There's plenty of work for all, but the competition is tough. Most of them go for a commercialised, rhythm-and-blues sound and they use material by people like Chuck Berry as a base for their own arrangements.'

I said, 'Do you remember the time when Berry's "Roll Over Beethoven" was issued and I went with Ringo Starr to buy the disc? It was a race to see which of our two groups could get their version out first and on the dance hall circuit.'

John said, 'Things are changing now. Before, if your music was good it didn't matter how you looked, but now presentation is beginning to play a big part.'

I argued that the sound was still the same, praising bands like King Size Taylor and the Dominoes ('really way out in the rhythm-and-blues field') and the originality of the Big Three.

'You see, what's happened,' Lennon continued, 'is that while down south you were experimenting with new sounds, we were working out new arrangements to old ones. At home we call it rhythm and blues with a Merseyside beat, but it's only now that it's beginning to pay off. The strange thing is that when the Beatles went south for a series of dates some time ago, nobody would listen to us unless we played hit-parade material. Now, of course, we can play our hits and more of our own compositions, but we still have to throw in one or two items from the hit parade.'

I said, 'I expect we'll have to do the same, yet at home if a rhythm-and-blues group does this, the kids accuse us of changing our style. But there is still a terrific swing towards Liverpool. To you, it might be just another trend, but to us it's the music we've been playing for four years. Whether or not it continues depends entirely on our ability to keep on creating new sounds.'

It was interesting to hear John Lennon talking about the

coming importance of presentation. In the early days, the Beatles didn't care a damn about how they looked at the Cavern. As Brian Epstein said, they were 'unkempt'. Never dirty, but smoking cigarettes and drinking Cokes between songs (the Cavern was unlicensed) and trading chat with the crowd. I was always much more aware of visual impact and we always looked smart. When Brian came along, he sharpened up the Beatles more than he needed to with us; but there was a brilliant piece of ammunition up the Beatles' sleeve that Brian recognised and he didn't need to do anything about.

Because Paul played bass guitar left handed, he and John were able to get their faces close up together at the microphone for the vocals, unlike most other players. So when they were singing, it was like a love affair with each other and the mike between them. So in every photograph you see of them they are tight together and the effect is very powerful. In those days, we didn't have a microphone each; we shared one, so for Macca to plan this effect for the Beatles, as I'm certain he did, was brilliant. I say this because Paul is and always was a shrewd mover and as a left-hander he was actually capable of playing a right-handed guitar with the strings strung in reverse. That is difficult, but Paul was too clever not to use his left-handedness to their advantage. He might deny it, but I'd never believe him on this: he capitalised on the situation and good luck to him. All the groups used to admire the look of the Beatles on stage and we'd say to each other, 'The bastard! Look what he's done! They look great, looking at each other singing. Fabulous!'

The girl who was to become my wife first caught my eye when I was playing with the Pacemakers at the Orrell Park Ballroom, Liverpool, in 1959. She was really pretty and I asked a friend to ask her for a dance and find out for me what her name was and where she lived.

A few nights later, we were playing at a club in a church hall at St John's, West Derby. This was run by Mona Best, Pete's mother; she also ran a cellar club called the Casbah at her home and was well known to all the local groups. The same girl was there; I'd seen her at the Cavern previously and always wanted to chat her up.

Pauline Behan (as she then was) was a huge Beatles fan before she was aware of Gerry and the Pacemakers. 'I thought the Beatles were absolutely fantastic,' Pauline says. She remembers Paul singing 'Lend Me Your Comb' when she first saw them at the Casbah – and that converted her from jazz. Of the individual Beatles, she was initially drawn to John Lennon.

Pauline takes up my story:

Gerry came over at the dance and knew my name. He said he got the same bus home as me. I wondered how he found this out, but he told me correctly that it was the 81 bus. I thought this was strange, as we didn't live in the same area. That was how he was: a real little con-man!

Did I want to get the bus home with him? I said yes, OK. I was with Linda Kermode, my best friend. Near the end of the dance he came over and said they'd decided to get a taxi, but would give me and my friend a lift home. The plan was to go through Hunts Cross (where I lived) first, then through Aigburth to drop off Les Chadwick, then to drop off Les Maguire at the Pier Head to catch the last ferry across the Mersey to his home in Birkenhead.

When it came to it, the trip happened in reverse, leaving Gerry taking me home, just the two of us. I was fuming. When the taxi stopped outside my home, as I got out, Gerry asked me for my phone number. But I was running up the path. It was late for those years – 12.30 in the morning. I knew my dad would be sitting waiting for me on the stairs.

I tried to get my key in the door and Gerry was shouting for my number from the taxi. I knew all the neighbours' lights would be going on and I didn't want to be the talk of the district. 'Tell me your phone number, shout it, I'll remember it,' he was yelling. I shouted it to silence him, thinking he'd never remember it.

Next night when I got home from my work (as a secretary at the Co-operative Building Society in Liverpool) my dad, whose name was also Gerry, said a boy named Gerry had been on the phone for me. When he called again and asked if I would go out with him, I agreed to go to the pictures. The night after that, he was playing a dance and I went. And it snowballed from there.

Pauline's memory is correct, but there was a difficulty in those early days. When I was pestering her for a date, she replied that her boyfriend was George Harrison of the Beatles. But he was in Hamburg at that time, so I decided that while the cat was away . . .

When he returned from Germany, George phoned her, said he was dying to see her again – and then, one lunchtime, as I was walking up the steps from the Cavern, Pauline was walking down. The Beatles were playing.

I said, 'Come on, let's have some lunch.' We'd been out a couple of times by then. But Pauline said she was going to see George. I returned alone downstairs to the Cavern and went to George.

'Hiya, Gerry,' he said.

I said, 'Don't smile. I've got some good news and some bad news. The good news is I'm in love. The bad news is that it's your girl.'

The conversation didn't last long. I think he said something to do with sex and travel. I then went back to Pauline upstairs and I told her there was no need for her to bother to go down – 'I've packed him in for you,' I added. Pauline was furious, but I've always believed in dealing with problems head on.

Pauline remembers:

George rang me that night and I said I was very sorry. He asked why I'd chosen Gerry Marsden, out of all the lads in Liverpool. George added, 'He's a flirt, you know.' I replied that he'd been a perfect gentleman with me.

There followed one final date between Pauline and George. He took her to the cinema and asked her to make a decision. She chose me, quite sensibly. But Pauline and George remained good friends and he often phoned her afterwards to ask how she was, if she was happy, which was nice.

When 'How Do You Do It?' went to the top of the charts, I was courting Pauline. I went in my Sunbeam Rapier to pick her up from work for lunch. 'I've got something to tell you,' I said as I drove her first to a fish and chip shop to collect some food and then to a seat in Sefton Park to eat it.

We sat down. 'Guess what?' I began. 'The record's gone to number one.'

'Oh my God, what does that mean?' she said. We were both just stunned. Then Pauline said, 'Blimey, wait till I tell my mum. What happens now?'

I told her that Brian Epstein and George Martin wanted me to make another record, but no matter what happened to it, when I'd made it, I intended to get a proper job. I think I said that because I was panicking. I was simply over the moon at the thought that I could really score a success in show business. After my second and third single, I said the same thing to Pauline about 'getting a real job', and it became a joke between us.

Brian Epstein still had his office above his record store in Whitechapel and all the groups were still knocking into each other there, talking about music – and now we had records of our own to discuss. The Beatles were going down the charts with 'Please Please Me' while I was enjoying the number one position, and I bumped into John Lennon chatting with another local musician, Steve Day.

'How does it feel to be Brian's number two group, then?' I asked him.

He obviously agreed with me, because he showed me two fingers! These were very early days. Pretty soon, Brian would have to move his office from Whitechapel to Moorfields to concentrate on being a manager, as he was signing up so many

Liverpool acts. He wasn't going to be able to run a record shop much longer.

The Beatles went to the top again with their third single, 'From Me to You'. The speed of it all seems crazy today. While 'How Do You Do It?' was being played to death on the radio, we went down to London to record another Mitch Murray song for our follow-up. Although I admired it, I wasn't so sure about this song, 'I Like It', because it had the same chords, the same feel as our first hit, but everybody felt it had a lively spirit that would do the trick. These were the years when a follow-up was generally considered to *need* the same ingredients as its predecessor. I told everyone I wasn't very confident, but was happy to be proved wrong. 'I Like It' went to number one within three weeks.

Mitch Murray says now:

Gerry was extremely creative with those first two songs of mine. He added a lot to them. It's rare that a songwriter lets a song go out to an artist and it comes back better than he could ever have imagined it. Usually, it's the other way round.

Mitch also recalls meeting me for the first time at a BBC radio 'Saturday Club' broadcast and says:

Gerry was a bit rude, hadn't got time to meet me. He thought I was the guy who sang on the demo for 'How Do You Do It?', but then someone explained I had *written* his first hit and he was totally different!

Now I don't speak to him at all!

Pauline asked me what I intended to do now I'd had success with my second single. I said, 'Make another, then pack it in and get a real job!' – which I have said ever since, after every record!

By mid-1963, things were going wild in Liverpool and in pop generally. Brian Epstein had signed other successful groups – the

Big Three had a hit with 'Some Other Guy' and Billy J. Kramer had a number one with 'Do You Want to Know a Secret?' – and the eyes of the whole country came down on Merseyside. Within six months, records by the Beatles, ourselves and Billy J. Kramer had sold more than two and a half million copies – and that came from only two singles, an EP and an LP by the Beatles, two singles by me and the Pacemakers, and Billy J.'s one single! We three groups posed for pictures together and the newspapers described us as 'the million dollar line-up'.

The money hadn't started to come in yet, but Brian promised it would eventually. He was already taking on too much work – later on, this side of his character would really damage him – but he had done such a lot for us in getting us record deals. Through his quiet style, Brian taught me how to deal with people. I sometimes went into his office in a fury, and he'd say, 'Sit down and let's have a chat.' I was a bit headstrong and he calmed me down.

He also smartened us up, sending us to the London showbiz tailor Dougie Millings who had designed the stage wear for pop stars for many years, people like Cliff Richard, Adam Faith, Eden Kane and the stable of acts managed by Larry Parnes (who was *the* manager of 1950s acts, as Epstein was of the 1960s).

Luckily, Brian Epstein, through his charm, latched on to the good people in the London music industry: George Martin, Ron Richards, Mitch Murray and Dick James.

Dick was already the Beatles' music publisher and he had a great sense of promotion. He started the ball rolling by getting us on the important TV and radio programmes. He took me to a Greek restaurant, introduced me to taramasalata and asked me if I would do these programmes to promote the records. Would I co-operate? 'Whatever you want me to do, Dick, it's in my interests and yours.' I could never understand why some acts were unco-operative in that promotional aspect. We later encountered a lot of people in show business who would bury people alive for a penny, but Dick was a truthful man who never fiddled anything from me. He formed Pacermusic to handle my song-publishing interests.

Cilla Black was a mate of everybody in the Cavern. I knew her as the occasional cloakroom girl. She also went to school with Pauline. Cilla was one of the lads in the best sense; we all liked her, and she was someone who was there at the start. She'd get up on stage and sing with anybody who would let her. She didn't have a great voice but she did have a personality that Brian Epstein recognised, and soon after he signed her John and Paul wrote her first record, 'Love of the Loved'.

When Brian Epstein decided he was going to try to launch Cilla as a singer, the Pacemakers and I backed her on a test tape made in an empty Cavern one afternoon: she sang 'Hallelujah I Love Him So'; 'Summertime' and 'Always'. Brian took the tape down to George Martin. Later on, Brian played me a song called 'Anyone Who Had A Heart', which had been made into a hit in the States by Dionne Warwick. He said he would give it to Cilla. I said that was lunacy; she hadn't got a great voice. I was a bit wrong. As he did with us, Brian saw a long-term future for Cilla as a family entertainer, and he was dead right.

Cilla has now found her true forte as a television personality, just as Brian Epstein predicted. She and her husband Bobby are dear friends of mine.

The bandwagon for Liverpool beat music, as it was so quaintly described by the rest of the country, became unstoppable once a few of us had hit the charts and the national papers began to interview us. Brian asked me if I'd like to go on tour with the Beatles, Roy Orbison, Sounds Incorporated and the singer Louise Cordet, who was having a hit with 'Just Like a Baby'.

It sounded great and I said yes. I remember being shocked when Brian said the tour would go around the cinemas and theatres. This was something we'd never experienced, touring the Odeons and Gaumonts in a 'package show'. We were told we'd each get twenty minutes on stage, and the old rivalry would begin to surface again, every act trying to get more applause than

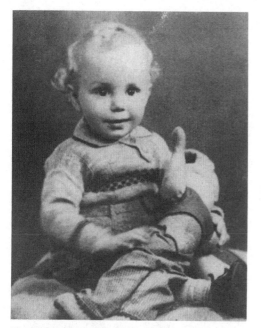

Young Gerry with his teddy: a child to break many a mother's heart!

With my mother and brother Fred on holiday in Great Yarmouth.

My parents and me. We've tried to smarten up for the photographer, but Dad hasn't got it quite right.

Above left: A very youthful-looking fourteen. I'm playing my Zenith guitar, my pride and joy in those years, at the opening of the Windsor pub in Liverpool.

Above: Me at fifteen, practising my moody Dean Martin look.

Left: Certificate of excellence awarded to the Gerry Marsden Skiffle Group by the Liverpool Youth Music Advisory Committee.

Above: Little Richard and me, again in Hamburg. Richard made the classic remark to me, 'One day you're gonna be a star but at the moment you're just a little light bulb!'

Left: Gerry and the Pacemakers at the Cavern.

Les Chadwick, Les Maguire, Bill Haley and Gerry Marsden in Hamburg. We all owe a lot to Bill and 'Rock Around the Clock'.

With Muriel Young on the TV show 'Five O'clock Club'. I can't remember why I decided to wash my face in front of the cameras.

'How Do You Do It?' was our first number one.

Above: Ringo Starr, John Lennon, George Harrison, Paul McCartney and me. I'd just said, 'Sorry, lads, I can't possibly join your band.'

Right: Shortly after 'How Do You Do It?' reached number one we toured Britain with the Beatles. This is our itinerary.

THE BEATLES
GERRY
AND THE PACEMAKERS

Merseyside's Two Chart-topping Combos Are Out On Tour Together!

MAY 18—SLOUGH, Granada
MAY 19—HANLEY, Gaumont
MAY 20—SOUTHAMPTON, Gaumont
MAY 22—IPSWICH, Gaumont
MAY 23—NOTTINGHAM, Odeon
MAY 24—WALTHAMSTOW, Granada
MAY 25—SHEFFIELD, City Hall
MAY 26—LIVERPOOL, Empire
MAY 27—CARDIFF, Capitol
MAY 28—WORCESTER, Gaumont
MAY 29—YORK, Rialto
MAY 30—MANCHESTER, Odeon
MAY 31—SOUTHEND, Odeon
JUNE 1—TOOTING, Granada
JUNE 2—BRIGHTON, Hippodrome
JUNE 3—WOOLWICH, Granada
JUNE 4—BIRMINGHAM, Town Hall
JUNE 5—LEEDS, Odeon
JUNE 7—GLASGOW, Odeon
JUNE 8—NEWCASTLE, City Hall
JUNE 9—BLACKBURN, King George's Hall

With Compliments from
Tony Barrow
Press & Public Relations Officer

John Lennon and me in 1963. He was a great mate. We all miss him.

With Hank Marvin and Bruce Welch of the Shadows, pretending we know what Châteauneuf du Pape is.

With Sammy Davis Junior at his fortieth birthday party at the Trattoo in London. A great pal, Sam, God bless him.

Cilla and me, about to get together under the mistletoe.

An early tour of the States with Billy J. Kramer and the Dakotas. We've linked up again many times for Sixties Revival concerts.

'Ferry Cross the Mersey' was a huge hit in the States, and remains the song I'm proudest to have written.

At the Brooklyn Fox Theatre in New York for one of the Murray the K concerts. I'm saying, 'I like it, hope you're liking it too.'

Me with the Pacemakers in the film *Ferry Cross the Mersey*.

programme

one	THE ROOFRAISERS
two	BRYAN BURDON
three	BOBBY SHAFTO
four	BRYAN BURDON
five	THE KINKS
	Interval
six	MIKE COTTON SOUND
seven	MARIANNE FAITHFULL
eight	GENE PITNEY
nine	BRYAN BURDON
ten	GERRY and the PACEMAKERS

In accordance with the requirements of the local authority: 1. All gangways, passages and staircases must be kept entirely free from chairs or any other obstruction. 2. The public shall be permitted to leave by all exit and entrance doors after each performance or entertainment. 3. No smoking shall be permitted to take place on the stage except as part of a performance or entertainment. 4. The safety curtain must be lowered and raised at least once during every performance or entertainment, to ensure its being kept in proper working order.

This programme is subject to alteration at the management's discretion   The taking of photographs is forbidden

The programme from one of the tours we did with other well-known sixties musicians. While we were on the road, 'You Really Got Me' reached number one and it seemed only right that the Kinks should top the bill after that.

the one before. It sounded just the sort of challenge I would enjoy. I told Brian I was intrigued. As the Beatles hit the top with 'Please Please Me' in the spring of 1963, Brian began his plans to put them and us together on this tour.

He had an excellent relationship with a Manchester promoter, Danny Betesh, who ran clubs where I'd played: the El Rio in Macclesfield and the Three Coins in Manchester. Brian and Danny had already planned for the Beatles to tour Britain on a bill topped by Roy Orbison.

'I want you to take my newest act on the tour, too,' Brian told Danny. 'Gerry and the Pacemakers – he's going to be a huge star; he has a new single coming out; he's really very, very good and he won't let you down.'

Danny remembers that he wasn't sure about putting me on a major tour. But when he asked Brian how much he wanted for me, Brian replied, 'Twenty-five pounds a night.' Danny felt he couldn't go wrong with that, and decided to put me and the Pacemakers on the tour, which was to begin on 18 May 1963 and last three weeks.

But by 3 April, I was number one with 'How Do You Do It?' and midway through the tour, my second single, 'I Like It', was released. Danny increased my pay to £250 a week (which worked out at forty-one pounds a night as it was a six-nights-a-week tour).

'It was still a bargain,' Danny says. 'Gerry closed the first half of the show and he went down very, very well.'

That was quite a turning point for the Beatles, too: the show had begun with Orbison as top of the bill, but it was quite obvious that the Beatles were not correctly positioned as second on the bill to anyone at that stage, such was the audience response. So Danny switched the billing; Roy Orbison, a perfect gentleman as well as a great artist, fully understood and accepted the position, which many other entertainers might not have done when faced with a change in status.

I felt a part of show business by now. The fans were screaming and pulling at our suits wherever we travelled. I remember one time when I was opening a fête in Liverpool: just as I had a shy at the coconuts, a group of girls ran up and tore my new suit to pieces. The kids tried to break into our rooms in hotels, and made it hard for us to come and go into the theatres, but we loved it all.

Several writers described me as the North's answer to Tommy Steele, which I considered a compliment. Then, just like now, I loved being on stage and in *Record Mirror*, Peter Jones wrote about me:

> Why is Gerry so popular? His own bubbling personality is a large part of the success. He works harder than most on stage and comes off pouring with sweat!

He pointed out that I was not typical of the Liverpool group scene because although we were called Gerry and the Pacemakers, we didn't rely on group vocals. I was more of a soloist. I was said to be 'out of the rut' of the other groups because I relied on my own voice to get a song across.

I was still living with my parents in the Dingle when we hit the top. Everybody in Liverpool knew where we lived and the streets were crazy with fans.

Letters were pouring into Menzies Street and also to Brian Epstein's office. He phoned Pauline at work and asked her to call in to discuss answering them. They were overwhelming him: he had neither the time nor the staff to cope. She did this, and answered thousands of letters with the help of her parents, who spread them out on the dining table after tea every night. Sometimes she'd work on the replies until 4 a.m.! But they grew to such a pile that Pauline couldn't carry the full sacks home any more. Brian asked if she'd give up her secretarial job and join his staff, because we'd already declared an official fan club with Pauline as president. But she refused to give up her work. The postman started delivering sacks to her home and she roped in girlfriends to help her deal with it.

This wasn't an easy experience for Pauline. She became very jealous about the sentiments of some of the letters from young girl fans, who sent all manner of things professing undying love for me: photographs, diaries, gifts, even panties.

Pauline says now:

Here was I, staying in night after night answering these letters, and knowing my boyfriend was being faithful to me . . . and then came a letter from a girl which set me thinking that she'd spent more time with him than just enough to sign an autograph. She wrote about things he'd been talking about.

When he came home, I'd wipe the floor with him, wanting to know everything about these letters. I'd say: who's this girl? How did you meet her? We'd argue, but my parents guided me through all this. Dad said to me, 'If I trusted anybody, I'd trust that lad. And you are very selfish. He's been on the road, he's tired, and you are moaning.'

As Pauline's dad pointed out, travelling the length and breadth of the country, recording our first album and doing TV and radio, it wasn't likely that I could be with a million girls who claimed in their letters that they had 'special relationships' with me.

We did hundreds of shows a year around Britain on concert tours with great American and British artists. We had great fun with pranks on the road during those one-nighters. One of the most typical was when we went round the country with Ben E. King, who had inspired us all so much with his hit 'Stand By Me'. Jimmy Tarbuck was the compère and as we set off for Scotland, we sent our road manager George Hollingsworth in a van ahead of the coach which carried the artists. This was only three days into the tour and Ben hadn't had time to get to know George. We told George to dress fairly seriously, flag down our coach near the Scottish border and pose as a customs officer.

As we got close to the border, we turned to Ben E. King and

said, 'Have you got your passport?' We knew he'd left it in a safe in his London hotel. No, he said, why would he need that? 'For Scotland,' we all told him. 'We're British, we don't need it, but you, obviously an American, won't get into Scotland without your passport.'

He started to panic. We worked on this, saying he'd have to stay in John O'Groats while we did the concert. He asked the driver to return to London for it, but we said there wasn't time.

Suddenly, in the countryside near the border, George Hollingsworth, dressed in a raincoat and hat, stepped out to flag us down.

'Bloody hell, Ben, here's the customs,' I said. He believed me.

'Right, everybody off the coach,' George said.

Jimmy Tarbuck whipped up the atmosphere. 'Bloody hell, this is trouble, we'll all be put in prison.' Ben believed everything.

'Anybody here foreign?' George asked.

'Yeah, Ben E. King,' we said.

'Why did you tell him?' Ben asked, agitated.

'Come on, by the colour of you and the way you speak, you're hardly from Liverpool.'

'Come on, guys, he's only little, I'll give him a punch,' said Ben, who was a hard case.

I said if he did that, we'd all be in trouble. These passport officers were trained as karate experts. I said the best way out of the difficulty was to talk to him nicely. We explained we were in show business on the way to our concert. George told us all that if we did an impromptu performance for him, singing, 'A Scottish Soldier' and 'Loch Lomond', he'd let us through as a favour.

'What are these songs?' Ben E. King asked. We wrote down the words, and there, on the roadside, were Jimmy Tarbuck, me and Ben E. King singing these Scottish songs to our road manager who was pretending to be a customs man. He then gave Ben 'permission' to enter Scotland.

As Ben was getting back on the coach, George asked him where he bought his shoelaces.

'New York.'

'You'll have to pay me twenty pounds import duty, because we allow only English laces into Scotland, I'm afraid.'

As well as paying, Ben took the laces off his shoes and handed them over. We arrived in Scotland and he was cursing, saying he had no laces; he wanted to kill the customs officer and lodge some sort of official complaint.

As we arrived at the theatre, we caught sight of George Hollingsworth driving up.

'Oh dear,' I said. 'There are problems if *he's* here again,' I told a now very angry Ben E. King. But I couldn't hold it any longer. 'By the way, Ben, this guy George is my roadie.'

Ben nearly killed Tarbuck and me. He went wild. But he got his money back. And after half an hour, he was laughing. Twenty years later, when Ben appeared on my 'This Is Your Life' programme, his entrance began with his singing, 'Ye tak the high road, and I'll tak the low road'. It was a wonderful episode in our memory.

3

Love and Marriage

Ferry Cross the Atlantic

When you walk through a storm
Hold your head up high
And don't be afraid of the dark.
At the end of the storm
There's a golden sky. . .

It really was the strength of those words that attracted me to
'You'll Never Walk Alone'. I first heard it when I went alone
to the cinema to see the film *Carousel* when I was a teenager.
The melody was beautiful, the dramatic effect was strong and
I immediately loved the sentiment of the message. I still do.

I'd introduced it into the act back in Hamburg days. The idea
was partly to provide a contrast with rock 'n' roll. The rest of
the band thought it was a strange choice at first but we worked
out a light beat, different from the soundtrack ballad version,
and I always loved singing it. Audiences were surprised, but it
was a difficult song for anybody really to hate.

The third record after two hits is tricky for an artist. After the
first, the second has a kind of impetus of its own. But the third
is notoriously a difficult choice: I didn't believe we could follow
the same formula of 'How Do You Do It?' and 'I Like It'.

Mitch Murray offered me 'You Can't Fool Me', which was
still in my style, but it didn't work well enough in the studio

to be the automatic decision. (Later, we put it on an EP.) Looking for my third hit, Ron Richards had conversations with another EMI producer, Norrie Paramor, who was in charge of Cliff Richard's recording career, and his assistant Bob Barrett. Ron was intrigued about how they had arrived at the decision to record Frank Ifield's huge number one hit, 'I Remember You'. They replied that Frank had revealed it was a favourite among his concert audiences.

When Ron asked me what went down well with my crowds, I told him 'You'll Never Walk Alone'. I was very keen on the idea of recording it because it was a way of broadening my range. I didn't want to be 'boxed in' to rock or beat; I loved ballads and still do, and I believed the scope of my career would improve if I pulled it off as a hit.

When we recorded the song with Ron Richards, he confesses now that he nearly had a heart attack at my treatment. It was, after all, one of the classic songs from a well-loved musical; when I reached the end and sang my own, halting breaks in the middle of the title, like 'You'll N-e-e-e-e-ev-e-e-e-rr Walk Alone', Ron was shocked. He thought, 'What *is* Gerry doing to this classic song?' Then he remembered the yodel which was the key to Frank Ifield's success with 'I Remember You-ooo' – and they all realised that I was giving the song a distinctive treatment.

Ron says now, 'I didn't say anything at the session, but if it had been a new song, I don't think I'd have let Gerry get away with it.'

In mid-1963, when we were putting together the first album, 'How Do You Like It?', it was natural that 'Walk Alone' should be included. It was great to hear myself singing with violins! When the time came for the third single to be chosen, I said to Brian Epstein and George Martin, 'I think that version is strong enough, and I think it will be a hit.' They both expressed concern. Brian, particularly, said, 'We want another number one from you and we just don't think that's strong enough.' George Martin and he finally agreed to make it my third single . . . but it was basically my risk.

In fact, it didn't strike me as such a dangerous move, musically. The charts were quite a mix at that time. Although the Beatles' popularity had gone wild, there were a few ballads around: Cliff Richard with 'It's All in the Game', Buddy Holly with 'Wishing' and Roy Orbison with 'Blue Bayou'.

I said 'Walk Alone' would do well, because it always went across well with the crowds. I had another reason for pushing it. I wanted to broaden my appeal inside the industry as well as with audiences. I knew that if I could get a hit with a ballad, it would open my career in the future towards cabaret. My roots would always be in rock 'n' roll, but I was telling Pauline and everyone that my ambition was to star in a West End musical. If 'Walk Alone' hit, I reasoned it would make people take me just a bit more seriously as an entertainer.

My old friend Frankie Vaughan commented on the record in the *Melody Maker*:

Absolutely marvellous. You wouldn't expect the song from Gerry, but he makes a great job of it. Imagine it – the beat world doing a ballad. But his diction is unmistakably Liverpudlian. His personality still comes across. I like this enormously. It has lots of charm and I'd say it stands a good chance.

To the surprise of a lot of people, 'You'll Never Walk Alone' became my fastest-selling single, a statistic that has remained. It roared into the top twenty at number eighteen on 12 October 1963. 'Gerry sets a hot pace,' said the chart headline. The following week it had gone to number seven, and it reached the top on 2 November, actually leap-frogging the Beatles who were at number three with 'She Loves You' and heading surely for their usually reserved position. It was great to beat my old mates. They did have the benefit of being on a gigantic British concert tour to promote their new record, and after two weeks at the top, 'You'll Never Walk Alone' was replaced by 'She Loves You' on 23 November.

That clinched for me an entry in the *Guinness Book of Records*, since that hat-trick of my first records going to number one has never been beaten. Interestingly, my fellow Liverpudlians Frankie Goes To Hollywood *equalled* my achievement with their first three singles in 1985 ... and the B-side of their number one hit 'Relax' was my composition 'Ferry Cross the Mersey'!

We may have been all mates from Liverpool tasting success, but on the record front, there was certainly a bit of rivalry about chart positions. The Beatles had not kicked off with three number one hit singles as I did, and according to Tony Barrow, who was the publicity director for Brian Epstein's stable of acts, 'what began as a very healthy artistic rivalry before 1963, became more bitter as time went by. It was two-sided – the Beatles were as jealous of Gerry as he was of them.'

With so many acts to juggle, Brian Epstein had to ensure that we all had a clear run at the charts and we didn't 'shoot each other in the foot' by having singles out at exactly the same time, preventing each other from reaching the top positions in the charts. All of the groups used to worry about this: 'Who else has a record out to compete with us?' And Brian would liaise with EMI to plan the release dates and promotion campaigns carefully. There was no point in competing head-on with the Rolling Stones, either, so Brian would consult with Andrew Oldham, their co-manager, on the same subject.

According to Tony, the black sense of humour that I shared with John Lennon was more acceptable from me than it was when John dished it out; apparently I was viewed as the 'rough diamond with a heart of gold', the shortish guy shooting my mouth off to compensate for my lack of size.

Looking back on the early 1960s, Tony says:

I think Gerry understood that Brian Epstein had to concentrate more time on the Beatles, but that didn't mean he objected to it any the less. He might have realised it was essential but I don't think that underneath it all, that understanding caused him to be any happier . . . there was always that bit of needle and resentment.

More to the point, it made the *group* unhappy, and it's important to remember that the Pacemakers and Gerry were a co-operative unit in those years. That's changed since, but back then, Gerry would take the stick from the group. The band often complained in my hearing that Brian Epstein wasn't in attendance at a concert 'yet again', and Fred Marsden would be riled particularly about that. I think Gerry softened it to them, and he didn't have any major rows with Brian because he appreciated his pressures, but it left Gerry as piggy in the middle.

At the NEMS office, there was a pecking order and being the second act signed by Brian, I had a seniority which Brian and most of the staff there recognised. The hierarchy was the Beatles, then me, then Billy J., then Cilla Black – but of course Cilla was different because she was not a group and not in the least competitive with any of us. So when a fan magazine rang Tony Barrow to ask for a comment by one of the Beatles, if they weren't available, then I was the automatic choice as the 'next in line'.

Brian had firm ethics about the way his company would handle us. Show-business managers in those years were notorious for 'trading off' their acts to their own benefit; for example, they'd say to booking promoters, 'You can have my big act for such and such a tour, but only if you give me so many thousands for this other act I have.' Epstein would never do that. We all had to make it on our own, without that sort of false boost. If Brian *had* operated like that, Cilla Black would have been a major success in America, because he could have used the success of the Beatles and me to ensure that she got a stronger exposure there. It's important to me to record the fact that my group made our impact alone, and not on the backs of the Beatles, and that was vital to Brian Epstein, too.

*   *   *

At the end of 1963, the ten number one discs that had sold the most during the year were all British. The best-selling list was:

1	She Loves You	The Beatles
2	I Want To Hold Your Hand	The Beatles
3	The Next Time/Bachelor Boy	Cliff Richard
4=	From Me To You	The Beatles
4=	You'll Never Walk Alone	Gerry and the Pacemakers
6	Confessin'	Frank Ifield
7	I Like It	Gerry and the Pacemakers
8	How Do You Do It?	Gerry and the Pacemakers
9	Summer Holiday	Cliff Richard and the Shadows
10	Diamonds	Jet Harris and Tony Meehan

Three hits within eight months did not make us rich overnight. Brian was paying us a set weekly salary and the rest went into the Gerry and the Pacemakers 'kitty'. For the first year or two of our success, we were too busy, still travelling quite a lot in the Liverpool area and racing around the country on those interminable package tours with Roy Orbison, the Beatles, Billy J. Kramer, Del Shannon, Ben E. King, Gene Pitney. It never stopped. We toured with the Kinks when their record 'You Really Got Me' was starting to happen – they were second on the bill to begin with but when their record jumped to number one, I said to Ray Davies, 'Right, Ray, you top the bill.' He was a bit shy about it, but they were a great band turning out classics, and they still are.

The money situation was a bit vague. It wasn't until two or three years after the hits that we had a few meetings with accountants, found for us by Brian, and started to learn about our income. We were too busy to spend much, anyway. I bought a new car, a P1800S Volvo, the same car I'd seen Roger Moore driving in 'The Saint' TV series; Fred bought an E-type Jaguar; Les Chadwick bought an Alfa Romeo; and Les Maguire a Mini Cooper S. I also bought a speedboat in Anglesey where my parents had caravans, but none of us went berserk because we believed the success would only last five years.

We never expected to make big money, so when we tasted success we got more of a buzz touring the world, meeting the stars whose music we'd always played, than sitting down counting our income. In those years, you bought something like a hairdressing salon or a garage or (in my case) an estate agency, and you thought that was your steady income set for life. We'd been working lads with no idea about investments. Lots went in tax.

The week 'You'll Never Walk Alone' went to the top of Britain's charts, I returned from a holiday in my beloved Anglesey in a buoyant mood. With the record all over the radio, people were expressing surprise at a Liverpool beat group doing such a well-established ballad. I felt chuffed.

But I also sensed a huge change around Liverpool, where I still lived with my parents when I wasn't charging around the country on one-nighters. The city's talent was drained dry. Record companies had sent their talent scouts to the city on just about every train from Euston, signing everything that moved. 'The groups we knew and had good times with in the Cavern don't have the same spirit any more,' I said rather sadly at the time. 'And the new ones that have come up have gone all big-time – they don't want to know you because they think they are stars themselves.'

Girl fans around the country were sending my favourite cough sweets backstage, together with giant scarves, fruit gums, hundreds of packets of crisps and even ice cream (all of which we said we liked during our interviews for teenage magazines). But in Liverpool, there was some resentment on the part of the original club regulars. We were getting letters of frustration from girls saying, 'Why did you ever make a record in the first place? Why don't you come back home?' There was a feeling of betrayal among the fans at the exodus by many to London. This was silly, really, because the best of us had always wanted to be successful nationally, and we were doing our bit for Liverpool. The tourists were starting to treat the Cavern like Buckingham Palace, something to come and stare at. Liverpool people, bless 'em, felt very possessive about us and, in their way, they didn't want to see the end of their special relationship with all of us. But I still lived in Menzies Street and I felt every bit as much a Scouser as I did before I became successful. I still do.

Despite having had three number ones, I was still determined to stay in the Dingle as long as possible, and as it turned out I remained there for a couple more years. People said to me, 'How come you've stayed and the bloody Beatles have deserted Liverpool and gone to live in London?' I said I really didn't want the hassle of moving to London; the Beatles were more famous than me and were more in the public eye. They needed to go.

Fans were knocking on the door of my home at all hours of the day and night, wanting autographs, and although it got to be a bit much, my mother was welcoming to every visitor. Many of the girls became family friends and my mother followed their lives into marriage, having children and so on. Not only that, but Mum expected me to remember all the details of the fans she wrote to, conscientiously, for years.

They'd consider her a friend, not Marsden's mother.

'Hello, Mrs Marsden, is Gerry in?'

'No, he's in America touring, but come in and have a cup of tea.'

I'd left a load of signed photographs, so she gave these out and took their names and addresses, adding, 'Now don't forget, he's back a week on Monday, so come and see him.' I was often told by Mum, 'Gerard [as she always calls me], those girls I told you about a fortnight ago have arrived.' Here I was, travelling Britain with number one hits, and my mother's calling me Gerard and the fans are sitting in my home having tea. They were gobsmacked!

She still does it, and I love it.

'Do you know Jennifer has had a baby?'

'Jennifer who, Mum?'

'Remember, the girl who came to our house in Menzies Street in 1965?'

I say, 'What!!'

And she'll continue, 'She came to see you but you didn't meet her for three weeks and she came back with a friend, Doreen. Well, she's had a second child.'

How the bloody hell am I supposed to know all this, I ask.

'Well, she still writes to *me*.' I'm supposed to follow the lives of these people exactly. 'Peter from Singapore wrote to ask when you're going out there.' She's still posting letters to these people after all these years. And it's great!

My parents kept me well and truly 'grounded' during those years. If I went home and swore, I'd get a strong reprimand from my mother. I still do. And I love that.

Cilla caught the temper of Liverpool people when she moved south for her career, too. 'She's left us, as well,' people said. Well, people do have to move on for the sake of their career, I'd say; but living in the Dingle suited me fine. Our fans thought I showed more loyalty to Liverpool than the Beatles and others, and in a way they were right.

I loved Brian Epstein. He had enormous charisma and his personality opened the door for many of us to our success. But he made a few mistakes. By the time I'd had three hit singles, the Beatles were enormous and he'd signed Cilla, Billy J. Kramer, the Fourmost, the Big Three and Tommy Quickly. And then in early 1964 he announced that he was moving to London. He was taking on too much and I told him so. 'Brian,' I said to him at his new office in Moorfields, 'you're going to blow the whole thing. The Beats and a couple of others are enough for one man. Don't overdo it.'

Brian's younger brother Clive, a delightful man, was helping him and Brian always assured me and everyone else that he would delegate a lot of the work. He didn't kid me; this was sheer rubbish. 'Brian, you wouldn't delegate the licking of a bloody envelope,' I said to him. 'That's the problem, and we're all going to suffer, including you.'

But he was on such a high he couldn't stop. On his trips to London, Brian was advised by some experienced show-business managers and agents that he should pull back, that the Beatles and one or two others were more than enough. The Grade Organisation even offered to buy Gerry and the Pacemakers from NEMS, and Brian called me in to his office. We were earning about £1000 a week at this stage as we roared around the country on concerts and started going into Europe.

'Truthfully, Gerry, I cannot devote the same time to the Beatles and yourselves,' Brian said, 'because the Beatles have become the biggest property Britain has ever known and you come second at this moment.' He added that the Grades would increase my income overnight.

Looking back, a sound business decision might have been to go with the Grades – Lew and Leslie Grade had great power, particularly in television, and would have been a good agency for me. But I didn't want to leave the Epstein umbrella, for two reasons. First, I trusted him. It later transpired that he was naive in business matters, but at least he wasn't a crook and there were plenty of those in show biz. (I exclude the Grades, of course.) Secondly, we were all part of a happy Liverpool family which had made such an impression on the entertainment scene. I didn't want to break that unity.

'I don't want any other management,' I replied. 'You've done what you've done for us with no problems. You'll just have to devote more time to the Beats, Brian, because they're so massive. I understand.' He loved loyalty and was thrilled with what I said, adding that in the long term he would continue to enjoy managing my career. I told him I wanted to appear in a stage musical and to Brian, who was a former acting student, this was interesting. He saw no reason why I shouldn't progress in that direction. He also saw Cilla as having a future in the theatre and he wasn't far wrong with both of us. It was good to have a manager who didn't just want to milk us dry as pop stars for as long as we could make hits – and then drop us, as a lot of them did in those years. Brian wanted real careers for all of us; alas, what I said to him about over-loading his stable was to prove to be true.

What annoyed me about Brian was that he could not see the wood for the trees. He missed opportunities, particularly in merchandising and concessions, for the Beatles. He should have been making billions more for the Beatles with Beatle soaps, Beatle rings, Beatle toilet paper. But he blew that. It didn't affect me financially, because Brian was honest, but it was crazy that he didn't hand that side of the business over to Clive, who had remained with the retailing arm of their company, selling electrical goods. It's a pity Clive didn't want to get involved in the show-business side in those years: he stayed in Liverpool with their father Harry, while Brian got so deeply into show business. If Clive had wanted to, he could have said, 'I'll manage Gerry, then,' while Brian coped with the Beatles. And that would have helped Brian.

But Brian had a problem handing anything to anyone.

'Brian, you must delegate,' I said to him.

'But what if it goes wrong?' he'd say.

'Brian,' I said, 'you never give it a chance to go wrong. You're gonna kill yourself.'

He had grandiose plans for touring. 'What I'd like to do,' he told me, 'is put tours out of all my acts simultaneously.' He wanted us all to headline our own, but I said we should all be on the same bill. 'The Beatles, Billy J. Kramer, Cilla and Gerry and the Pacemakers all on the same bill right round the world. How could there ever be a better tour? It's staring you in the eyes!' I told him. 'We've all had number ones. It will be big.' No, he said, he wanted us all to have our own tours, each top of the bill in our own right.

This was sheer madness and I told him so; apart from the Beatles, none of us could headline tours all round the world. But together we'd make megabucks. We would have slayed the world as a touring package of that calibre. Why pay money to add acts from other management organisations to his own, when he had so many? But you couldn't persuade him. I'd leave the office saying, 'Sod it, Brian' . . . and because I liked him so much, I'd end up apologising.

Everybody in the management stable, particularly Paul McCartney who took an interest in Beatles business, warned Epstein that it was getting out of control and he was taking on too many artists. I said to him so many times, 'This is getting stupid.' On one occasion, I mentioned an act to Brian and he said, 'Who are they? Is that a new band?' I said, 'Thank you, Brian, for proving my point. You are their *manager*! Look, you don't even know what you've got!'

He was so naive, but you couldn't get through that brick wall. He once asked me to move to London, saying I'd get more television work, which was true. But I refused. I said if moving to London was the only way I could get television, I'd rather not have the work. I preferred to stay in Liverpool. He never raised the matter again.

I also told Brian at that decisive meeting that I could probably only expect five years of big earnings. Because of that, I wanted investment advice.

'Don't talk to me about money because I don't know about it,' he answered. 'Get yourself financial advisers. I'm useless in looking after money.' So I did. In money affairs, Brian was certainly an honest fool.

At Christmas 1963, I inched towards my ambition when, with the Pacemakers, I starred in a pantomime, *Babes in the Wood*. We took the roles of the Wandering Minstrels in the show at the Gaumont, Hanley. Brian Epstein promoted the show, in association with the impresario Joe Collins, father of Joan and Jackie. I enjoyed this step in the right direction.

In the spring of 1964, Pauline and I decided to get engaged. When I went to tell Brian Epstein, I was shocked at his reaction. He felt this could be bad for my career. A big proportion of my popularity was among teenage girls, he said, and it was important to keep alive for them the fantasy of my 'availability'.

This old-fashioned attitude about pop stars and their fans sounded ridiculous to me. A lot of the lads in all the groups had regular girlfriends and everyone in Liverpool had always known it. Brian had already tried to hush up John Lennon's marriage to Cynthia back in August 1962, without much success. I think Brian was concerned also because he was on the verge of moving his headquarters to London and didn't want to risk the whole pack of cards falling in on him with adverse publicity.

He'd just come back from America, where the Beatles had appeared on the Ed Sullivan TV Show to start their staggering success in the States. He probably did not want to risk my marriage losing us fans in that important market. He had a lot on his mind, and Gerry Marsden getting engaged was just too much.

He called Pauline to his office alone. 'It would be to Gerry's advantage if he remained single in the public eye,' he told her, so if we did want to press on with the engagement, could it please remain a secret. Pauline was surprised and upset. As things turned out, I was able to come up with a compromise solution.

I'd recently met Cliff Richard, who had just returned from the Canary Islands, where he'd filmed *Summer Holiday*. He was raving about the place, so I decided to take Pauline there for our first holiday away together. It was the first time Pauline had been in a plane. Before we went, a jeweller went to Pauline's house with a selection of rings; we didn't want to go anywhere in public to choose one. Pauline recalls how frustrating it was when I told her she couldn't wear the ring, and I took it back home.

We got engaged quietly in Las Palmas and before the journey home, Pauline removed the ring and placed it on a chain around her neck. Back in Liverpool, she told Brian that this pretence was farcical since everyone knew John was with Cynthia. But Eppy said the Beatles were in a special position because there were three others to carry such publicity, to divert people's attention. 'Gerry is different. He's the star.'

Eventually Brian agreed and we became officially engaged on New Year's Eve, 1964.

* * *

The year 1964 had opened very happily for me. I had recorded a song I'd written, 'I'm the One', and George Martin liked it enough to make it the topside of our new single. After three successes, it was a nerve-wracking time.

Reviewing the record in the *Melody Maker* that January, John Lennon said:

> It's a hit, of course. I like this. I like the beat. Sounds a bit like 'Night has a Thousand Eyes'. The thing about this is that Gerry has written it and he wanted badly to write an A-side. He kept writing B-songs. This isn't for my record collection, but then neither is 'She Loves You', really. 'I Want To Hold Your Hand' is, though. I like that.

The record went to number two, kept off the top by another great Liverpool group, the Searchers, with a really fine record which has stood the test of time, 'Don't Throw Your Love Away'.

We had a hell of a lot of fun on the road. Travelling around Britain by coach on those one-night-stand package tours, with some great artists, the feeling was truly happy-go-lucky. All the artists considered themselves equal – but on one of our first tours, we became irritated by Del Shannon. He'd enjoyed big hits with 'Runaway', 'Swiss Maid' and 'Hats Off to Larry', and we thought he was a bit snooty and big-headed. He was the American superstar and we were kids from Liverpool, and somehow he let us know it. I said to the band, 'I'll change his attitude somehow.' When the travelling show hit London and we went back to our hotel, we persuaded him to have a drink. We were ready to drink all night but shortly after we got to the lounge, at two in the morning, Del said he was going to bed. I said, 'No, stay. Join the party!' But he huffed and puffed and in his stand-offish way went to his room.

We were young and could stay up drinking in those days. At 5 a.m. I said to the Pacemakers, 'Mr Shannon is going to get to like or hate these boys from Liverpool.' I went to his room, knocked, and he said in an angry, sleepy way, 'What do you want?'

I assumed a very English accent and said, 'Mr Shannon, there's a telegram here for you.'

He rasped back, 'Put it under the door', with a few expletives thrown in.

I said, 'I'm sorry, sir, but you'll have to sign for it.' So he came out of the bedroom with these incredible boxer shorts with spots on, that the Americans always seemed to wear in those years. At that point, I dragged him clear of the door and slammed it.

'What *are* you doing?' he asked, standing outside the door.

I said, 'I'm doing nothing, but *you're* going downstairs in those shorts to get another key to your room from the night porter. And this will remind you that from now on, you're gonna *talk to us*.' He was OK from then on, and became a very dear friend. We toured with him on his final British tour before he died.

In the spring of 1964, when it was time for a new single to be cut, my thoughts turned to a song I'd written in Hamburg four years earlier. I'm a romantic devil at heart and I liked writing and singing ballads, which the German audiences did not expect. I told them to 'kiss, cuddle, do what you like' to the change of tempo from the rock 'n' roll they were used to. My wish to write ballads was based on the interesting fact that there was *so* much good rock 'n' roll stuff from the other singers; therefore I looked for a contrast.

It was an argument with Pauline that inspired one of my most popular ballads. During this argument, she said, 'Right, that's the end, we are finished' and I wondered how I was going to get her to come back to me. It was before we were married. Lying on my bunk bed in the flat on the Grosse Freiheit, I saw a beam of light coming through a hole in the curtain. I don't know why the phrase occurred to me – probably a mixture of emotions were running through my mind – but I remember thinking, 'Don't let the sun catch you crying.'

I said to myself, 'God, that's a nice title.' The Pacemakers couldn't figure out what I was talking about, but I got up and went over to the Star-Club where we were appearing, sat down and wrote it with my guitar there and then; it was featured in the show that night.

As it seemed so appropriate, I taped the song and then sent it to Pauline. Two days later she rang me and said, 'Gerry, let's get back together again.' Do you know, some days I wish I hadn't written the bloody song!

It was one of loads we had written and though I liked it, I wasn't certain about its commercial prospects. But when we were preparing albums, George Martin and Brian Epstein enthused about it, predicting that it could be a big hit in the United States.

'Don't Let the Sun Catch You Crying' became my fifth British single release in April 1964, on the eve of the first American tour. Although it didn't get to the top, it reached number six just as we landed in New York. It was exciting; America was a distant, impossible dream in those years and I could hardly get over the accents and the amazing size of the skyscrapers. All we knew of the States was from films; it was unbelievable to be mobbed by hundreds of screaming teenagers at the New York airport which they'd just re-named John F. Kennedy airport after the murder of the US president six months earlier. Murray the K, the disc jockey who was becoming famous with the 'British Invasion', met us and interviewed us. Although we were known by the fans who were watching the British scene carefully, we had not yet had a hit in the States and I was most anxious to secure a foothold. Reporting on its front page that 'Gerry and the Pacemakers had set the city jumping', the *Melody Maker* said that our riotous reception and crazy scenes were reminiscent of the Beatles' earlier reception. We went with Brian Epstein to our hotel, the Americana, and later took in the sights of New York. 'Don't Let the Sun' was our first US hit, reaching number six.

There was wild audience reaction when in May 1964 we

performed on the influential Ed Sullivan coast-to-coast TV show; we sang 'I'm the One' and 'Don't Let the Sun Catch You Crying'. The *Melody Maker* added that the critics considered us 'the best of all British beat visitors so far for showmanship', and we returned to the show the following week.

Just before we left Britain, we'd played the Opera House in Blackpool on the same bill as Sammy Davis Junior. In my New York hotel suite the phone rang and a voice said, 'Hi, Gerry, this is Sammy.'

I said, 'Sammy who?'

He said, 'Sammy Davis Junior,' and I said, 'Oh get stuffed' and slammed the phone down, believing it was a hoax. He called again and I said, 'Whoever that is, stop ringing this number.'

'Gerry,' he insisted, 'we just played the Opera House in Blackpool together. It's *me*!' I was shocked that he'd found me and bothered to call. He invited the band and me to the Copacabana where he was appearing and we had a wonderful reunion. He was a superb entertainer, and a very, very nice man!

Touring the States, appearing on the TV 'Shindig' show and playing places that we'd only heard about from American singers visiting Britain, we were in at the start of a colossal British domination of the American teenage scene. That year, 1964, saw the triumph not only of the Beatles, us and the Rolling Stones, but a whole army of groups like the Animals, Herman's Hermits and the Dave Clark Five.

Murray the K was a big Manhattan name, a 'happening' disc jockey on the radio and a lively compère. He befriended the Beatles and most of the touring British groups. We all appeared on his radio show. I went on and, like all Murray's guests, I was asked to read commercials. I did one for a night-club in which one of the lines read, 'If you're the kind of person who knows what to do but can't find the place to do it . . .' at which point I ad-libbed, 'Come up to our hotel later.' Murray and our fans thought this was funny, but I've no idea if the night-club people heard it.

In 1965 I was booked for the important Murray the K Easter Show at the Fox Theatre, in Brooklyn, New York. This was a tough one. During the afternoon shows, we'd see a few white faces in the audiences, but at nights they were all black, and they were no walk-over. The day shows were great, but the nights were murder. This was a baptism of fire into America, because the crowd wanted the black sound. With 'Ferry' riding high, I was top of the bill of twelve acts, all black except us. And what a cast it was: Marvin Gaye, Smokey Robinson and the Miracles, Martha and the Vandellas, the Temptations, the Four Tops, the Marvelettes, the Righteous Brothers (who had a huge hit with 'You've Lost That Lovin' Feelin'), Little Anthony and the Imperials, the Rag Dolls, the Del Satins (who did the American version of 'Sweets for my Sweet', popularised in Britain by the Searchers) and Cannibal and the Headhunters. Even if such a cast was bookable today, it would cost millions!

Murray made a lot of money from us, but he also did a great promotional job, so I didn't mind. John Lennon did take it to heart that Murray the K made money from us groups.

We also went on the road for long, hard tours – once with Sonny and Cher – on buses with beds in them. I hated them. It was horrendous and I was glad when we moved up to flying to and from the cities.

I was delighted when Ann Wilson, a true supporter, came to me during one tour of the States to ask if she could form a fan club. She had seen me for the first time on 'The Ed Sullivan Show' and remembers how I first made an impression on her: 'Here was this marvellous, cheeky, wonderful voice,' she says, 'dead sexy, everything you could possibly want in a young male vocalist – and what got to me was the fact that Gerry waved to Dusty Springfield when she was off stage; Dusty had been on the same show. I thought it was a marvellous, spontaneous gesture that the Beatles would not do!'

Ann took over the fan club after coming home from seeing the movie *Ferry Cross the Mersey* three or four times in one evening, which qualifies her for some kind of medal for bravery.

She did a great job for me and as the years went by I got used to the surprise of seeing Ann turn up at the most unexpected moments at my shows in Britain: suddenly, there she would be, sitting in the front row centre as I looked out from the stage.

In our early years, the thought of becoming popular in the States was out of the orbit of British rock 'n' roll bands like mine. But Ann thinks our very Englishness was an important part of the attraction. She's on record as saying:

> One of the Pacemakers once said to me: 'Gerry's not a good guitarist.' I thought about it and realised I *could* hear him missing notes, but I really don't care ... Gerry's singing, his whole stage presence and his emotional personality are what stand out for me.

Ann also detected that I was apprehensive of the American audiences. 'He was so English,' she says, 'you couldn't really grasp what it was about Gerry's concerns over America. It didn't turn me off, it intrigued me. I realised I had an even harder job to do, convincing him that his fans were here to stay.'

Ann began collecting some letters from fans which told in quite moving terms just why we had made our marks with them on our tours.

'Gerry seems to take as much delight in watching the audience as we take in him,' wrote Beth Morgan of San Francisco. 'He was constantly scanning the audience.'

Pat Helsel of Pittsburgh wrote: 'G is for the good looks you possess, E for the excitement you bring, R is for the records you sell, R is for the rate at which they sell, Y is for the youth that love just you.'

An amusing story came from Elaine Zurbrigg, recalling our concert at Toronto, Canada, in November, 1964:

> During half-time at the concert my chum and I were invited to their dressing room. Unfortunately police security wouldn't

let us into their room. Unknown to us, though, was the fact that Gerry had put on a custodian's uniform and had taken a broom and was nonchalantly sweeping the halls of the Maple Leaf Gardens where he and his boys were performing. Hundreds of girls were pressing at his dressing-room door trying to get a glimpse of him while he was sweeping the floor in the midst of us, unrecognised.

I always spring to life and feel cheerful when I'm on stage and I'm sure it was mainly this liveliness that made such an impact with our audiences the world over. Particularly in America, where so many artists seem to take making music rather too seriously; in my book, it should be fun and I, like the audience, have gone to have a good time.

One fan wrote to sum up that response rather well:

You probably have millions of love letters, but this isn't one of them. I want to tell you exactly why I like you and your music. You're *you*. When I see you on stage, in TV and in the movies, you act normal and not 'put on'. So many of the groups act so weird, but you don't. I can tell you're a clean-cut English guy and so do many girls. This is why you are popular in America.

That was from Mary Gasik in Harvey, Illinois.

'I love Gerry,' wrote Hilary Kest of the Bronx, New York, 'because he is not handsome to most people but he is to me. When he smiles everything in me feels good. When I feel sad, I look at him and then I feel better.' If ever I wanted a reason for getting on stage, it was summed up in that sentiment.

I was still only twenty-two when all this was happening. Not surprisingly, I became super-confident. I remember coming back from the US tour feeling that at last I was a superstar. After just a few hits! But I reckoned without the stabilising influence of my parents. I walked through the door back in Menzies Street and my mum told me to clean my shoes. That's a big thing in our house: Dad maintains that a man will always be judged by the cleanliness of his shoes, even if he's wearing old trousers or jeans.

My parents and family always helped me keep my feet literally on the ground and I've appreciated that leveller, because show business could have been heady for a guy travelling the world at such a young age. They might only have been able to afford a terraced house in Dingle, but by God it was spotlessly clean inside, the front step was always immaculate and the brass was always shining. That was why I wanted the band to look smart, because I was told by my parents that how I looked reflected back on them. That feeling has never left me.

We made quite an impact on America. Because of the success of 'Don't Let the Sun Catch You Crying', the US fans went out and discovered that we'd made earlier singles they hadn't heard about. That sent our first British hits, 'How Do You Do It?', 'I Like It' and 'I'm the One', into the American chart.

When we got back from America, we were amazed to find that, far from making a profit, we owed people there a total of three thousand dollars. We'd been given the red carpet treatment – limousines, fancy hotel suites – and taken people on the trip who were not necessary, plus the press party. And there were lavish restaurant trips.

When we asked Brian Epstein when the money from the US tour would come in, he said we 'didn't make that much money because . . .' and then he produced this list of staff who'd travelled, car rental charges, people we had paid to entertain over there – but about whom we knew nothing! I hit the roof.

'This is bleeding stupid,' I said to him in the language he often described as 'salty'. 'Never again,' I said. 'Next time we go to the States it's me and the band and you if you want to come – and they can supply the cars. We don't need a limousine each!'

It was the same in Australia. But we were innocents abroad the first time round, getting such a thrill from seeing the world that questioning the finances came as a second thought. It was only later, when we got money through royalties via the Performing Right Society, that we realised our records had made us some money. But that took a few years.

So much success had come to me, and many other Liverpool stars, so quickly, that we were almost bound to show some effects. I was always super-confident of my show and nerves had never been a problem, but for my first appearance at the London Palladium in 1964, I experienced what is still the only crack in my behaviour during my thirty years in the business.

In those years, an artist's 'arrival' at the London Palladium was a pinnacle, one of the highest accolades in show business; and my appearance on the celebrated ITV weekly programme 'Sunday Night at the London Palladium', a year after scoring three number-one hits in a row, caused me to be a bag of nerves throughout the day of the show. In fact, I went missing for some hours and Brian Epstein phoned everyone in our party, including Pauline who was staying at the Kensington Palace Hotel, to ask if I had been 'sighted'. Finally they found me – in the men's room at the Palladium.

The show went smoothly and afterwards Brian threw a party for which he hired a suite at the Grosvenor House Hotel. Some friends, as well as my parents and Pauline, had come down from Liverpool for the big day.

After the show, like every artist who's ever been on a stage, I needed an hour or so to 'come down' from the rush of adrenalin that had lifted me to dizzy heights that day. However, this wasn't to be. Pauline remembers the events of that extraordinary night very well:

Gerry was very quiet, sitting next to me on a settee, and there was a certain person employed by Brian whom Gerry was not very keen on; this man was making digs at Gerry and this caused Gerry to feel on edge after a difficult day. Gerry told me he was going to jump up and hit this bloke to get his revenge. He was behaving very strangely, with after-show nerves, and seemed totally out of character.

I said to Brian, 'For goodness' sake speak to him,' and as I started to get up from the settee to try to calm down Gerry, Brian was holding me back, telling me to leave him alone. With that, Gerry turned to me with a look in his eyes I'd never seen before and as he came over to me, he said he wanted to take me away from the party. I told him to behave himself, stop being stupid, but he began chasing me round the settee. It wasn't anything nasty, we were all laughing and joking about it, but I asked Brian again and again to deal with him, make Gerry sit down. Brian said, 'Pauline, please, just keep moving, because any second now he's going to flake out.' I had no idea what Brian meant, but this behaviour went on for quite a while. Eventually, Gerry literally fell into an armchair and passed out.

We put Gerry to bed in the bedroom of the suite and got one of his friends to stay with him. We all then went home. As Brian drove me back to my hotel in Kensington he said to me,

'Tomorrow morning, go back to the Grosvenor House to see him, but I want you to promise me you will never, ever mention anything about tonight and how he behaved.'

I replied, 'I *will*. I'm going to wipe the floor with him!'

But Brian insisted, 'Pauline, he won't remember any of it, so there's no point in bringing it up.' I asked Brian if he knew what had happened and whether he'd experienced it before.

He said he had and that it was a type of breakdown after a big show that he had seen before. Brian continued his story by saying it was not a nervous breakdown but a reaction. He said nobody could take the shock of what they were experiencing, of being a kid in Liverpool with no money and then suddenly having all that fame and fortune. It was too quick for anybody to handle without something snapping. I can't say he was drunk, even though I was blaming drink for it; Gerry had had a few drinks, but he could take a whole lot more than he'd had before he gets drunk, so that was very doubtful. Brian insisted that the brain could only take so much and in such a short time Gerry had to learn to handle himself so professionally at the Palladium that he deserved to show a little crack in himself.

Next morning, I was flying back to Liverpool to return to work; Gerry and I were not yet married. Brian picked me up to go and visit Gerry at his hotel, and on the way he repeated his instruction that I was not to mention the previous night.

'He'll be like a newborn puppy today,' Brian added.

When we knocked on the door of his hotel room, Gerry answered it full of beans and he never once mentioned the events of the previous night. It was several years before we discussed it. If anyone had said to me that Gerry might go to pieces, I'd have said, no way, because he's not that sort of person. But this was very different, some kind of Palladium nerves and thankfully Brian knew how to handle the situation because it was quite frightening at the time.

I don't remember a thing about all this, of course, but I'm in no position to deny it!

With a successful American trip behind us, Brian Epstein had been pursuing the idea of moving me on from rock 'n' roll into the film world or the theatre. It was a bit early, but he was friendly with Tony Warren, the creator of the TV series 'Coronation Street', and Tony had an idea for a feature film based on the Liverpool ferries.

I'd always been a ferry user and ferry watcher, right from my days as a van delivery boy; the ferries were, and still are, a vital part of the atmosphere of Liverpool. So I was very interested. They said I had to take part in the film and write a load of songs. In those days, it sounded easy. I said, 'Great. No problem. I'll get to work.'

Ferry Cross the Mersey was a video before videos were invented. Brian Epstein thought the film should have as many songs in it as possible so it could be seen in the States, Canada, France and everywhere as well as Britain, mostly as a showcase for us as performers.

There was a little storyline by Tony Warren, which had me living on one side of the Mersey, crossing to the other to go to art college (shades of John Lennon), forming a band and playing around Liverpool until a man came up with a talent competition. We entered it and naturally won and became famous.

There was a lot of knockabout comedy, but the film was mainly a vehicle for the nine songs which I wrote with the Pacemakers. These were performed in ridiculous situations for fun. We would sing in Chinese restaurants when suddenly a piano would appear; on the ferry a piano appeared; in the middle of the street a piano would appear – mainly it was an excuse for songs. But it was also a pre-video age video to show our faces around the world in countries where we couldn't tour, because we were too busy to tour everywhere. I fell in love and kissed a girl (that was as much as you could do in a movie in those years); Julie Samuel played that part; George Scott was the undertaker; Eric Barker was Julie's father; T.P. McKenna was Brian Epstein and Mona Washbourne was my Aunt Lil.

It was filmed in and around Liverpool and in Elstree. It should have taken a day and a half to make, it was so simple, but it took three months. I still bump into people who thank me for giving them work as extras who earned five pounds from that film.

Though it was not really a strong story it worked well enough in its way for the period. Pop stars weren't expected to make 'significant' films, and I suppose it was roughly in the vein of Cliff Richard's *Summer Holiday*. Well, I never said it would be better than *Ben Hur* or *Cleopatra*. It was such a great film they never made another; who would want to spoil the memory of the original!!!

The songwriting difficulty came when they said the title song was to be called 'Ferry Cross the Mersey'. I asked if it could be 'Ferry *Across* the Mersey', which would have been easier, and which is how we spoke about the boats – you took a ferry across to New Brighton – but they said no.

It was a challenge. I used to go down there with Pauline and stare at the boats and try to get inspiration. Nothing worked. It didn't come for several months. Then, one night, I was taking Pauline out for dinner. I picked her up in Hunts Cross where she lived and we were going to Southport. In my head as we drove I heard the opening notes of the song.

As we passed the ferry boats, I thought, 'Wow, that's it.' I stopped the car, jumped out and phoned my mother. I told her to put the tape-recorder to the phone and I hummed the tune into the tape. Then, returning to the car, I told a rather speechless Pauline that our dinner date would have to be cancelled.

I turned the car round, went straight home, dashed into the parlour, put the tape-recorder on and completed the soundtrack song for *Ferry Cross the Mersey* in about three minutes. Words and music were done together on a song I'd been trying desperately for three months to construct. I think Pauline agreed that the cancelled dinner was justified.

The best songs usually come that way. I'm not a song factory and I can't churn them out like a machine. I need a little bit of inspiration – the shaft of sunlight for 'Don't Let the Sun', the sight of the ferries for 'Ferry' – and driving near the Mersey that evening in 1964 definitely proved it. I tell Pauline that if she was sad about missing dinner that night, my whole family have eaten well from 'Ferry' ever since.

Being asked to write a song based on the ferries was one of those moments of luck in life that everybody enjoys. I always felt passionate about the ferries. When I was growing up, the overhead railway was brilliant, but that has gone. The ferries were always a vital part of Liverpool and I could never imagine the city without them. It was a tragedy that the overhead railway was dismantled – typical of what modern planners thought of as a way of building a 'better' city. That never works in any city, and in a place with Liverpool's special atmosphere, the old characteristics should be left alone.

In the early 1980s, the ferries were under threat of closure and I was glad to help in the campaign to keep them. The battle's never over because they always need more money, but I've become associated with Friends of the Ferries to fight to keep the ferries alive.

I'm proud to be only the second person in history to receive the Freedom of the Ferries – and I'd love to know who the first one was. It means that my family and I can use the ferries free for ever. I hope they keep running. As the ferries pull into the Pier Head, they play my song and to me that's a thrill money can't buy. I campaign and appear to help the ferries when I can. Liverpool needs those ferries for ever. If we lose such a vital part of the city's history, especially now that the port is not strong as it used to be, then we've got nothing.

The single didn't get to the top – at year's end, 1964, it reached number eight in Britain and six in America – but it became a special kind of record, part of my trademark. Every performer and songwriter strives for this: to have written something that means something to him, that carries a message, and even if it wasn't a chart-topper first time round 'Ferry' is now one of the most popular songs in my concerts around the world.

There were some tender moments in the film that touched a nerve in American audiences, and some fans wrote very enthusiastically about it. One, Wayne Lawless of Woodburh, Oregon, wrote:

A twenty-three-year-old male belongs to the Gerry and the Pacemakers fan club. Why? I was talking to a friend and mentioned that I was a member of the Judy Garland fan club. He nodded and agreed that Judy is an extraordinary show lady. Then I mentioned that I belonged to the Gerry and the Pacemakers fan club. 'You crazy or something? That's for teenagers, and teenage girls at that.'

Listen, my friend, I said. I am well aware of the appeal Gerry and his group hold for teenage girls. Gerry is a very good-looking guy and can send girls into a tizzy when he winks his eye right at them. But there is more to Gerry and the Pacemakers than good looks and sex appeal, and the teenage girls know this, as well as their parents, and even *their* parents!

They are young men who have a way with a song. They know how to sing and play it in order to bring out everything that the song must possess. They can even make a bad song sound good.

Luckily, *Ferry Cross the Mersey* was playing in town that day. I talked him into seeing it. As we left the theatre he smiled and said, 'Do you have the address of the fan club of Gerry and the Pacemakers?'

I asked him what convinced him.

'It was the scene, in Gerry's bedroom, when he took the picture of Julie Samuel [his girl in the film], placed it on his knee and sang "She's the Only Girl for Me".'

Ferry Cross the Mersey was much more popular in the States than in Britain. When I go to Beatles conventions there to speak and play, they ask me to do 'Why Oh Why?', the words of which I've long forgotten.

In the States, 'Ferry Cross the Mersey' was released ahead of the Beatles' 'Penny Lane', and of course everybody pointed out that Liverpool's top two groups were singing about their city. Ann Wilson's theory about the difference between the two treatments is interesting:

'Ferry' is emotional, whereas 'Penny Lane' is more of a celebration. The contrast in the songs they wrote of Liverpool tells you a lot about the difference between the two bands: with Gerry, it's always the emotional warmth, and that came across very strongly in 'Ferry', which is why it did so well in the United States.

That song and 'Don't Let the Sun Catch You Crying' are my biggest American successes, whereas of course in Britain, 'You'll Never Walk Alone' has the distinction of being a football-ground anthem.

Pauline bought me a book called *The Book of the Worst Films Ever Made*, because I love watching black and white 'B' films on television, preferably horrendous ones that cost thirty pounds to make. When I went through this book, I was thrilled because it contained all the films I loved to watch . . . and there's a section of trash pop films including *Ferry Cross the Mersey*. *I've made it!* Pauline was surprised, but that's a big buzz for me with my sense of the ridiculous.

The title song, though, will always be very special to me. I love the sentiment of the song about my home city.

So Ferry Cross the Mersey
  'Cos this land's the place I love
  And here I'll stay . . .

I still mean every word of it. As my fan club president Phil Tucker has written:

Many Liverpudlians left Merseyside when they found fame, but Gerry has always remained there, loyal to his city and his background. He becomes very passionate when talking about Liverpool. You can take Gerry out of Liverpool and across the globe, but you'll never take Liverpool out of Gerry.

Brian Epstein was charming and Pauline was fond of him, but he was still very concerned about the effect our marriage would have on my fans. But by mid-1965, many musicians in Liverpool were getting married. It was the end of that era, the start of a new one for so many, and we persuaded Brian to give us his 'permission'. He was among a hundred guests at our wedding at St Mary's Church, Woolton, on 11 October 1965.

We didn't have a honeymoon. We married on a Monday and fooled people by saying we were going out of the country straight away. But Liverpool football club were playing Juventus in the European Cup on the Tuesday and I couldn't miss that. The Liverpool manager, Bill Shankly, who had become a close friend since the Liverpool fans had adopted 'You'll Never Walk Alone', didn't expect us to attend and was amazed when Pauline and I showed up.

'I thought you were on honeymoon,' he said.

'So did I,' I said.

Then we came back to the house and locked ourselves in for a while; we weren't bothered because everybody thought we were away.

We had bought a house in Caldy on the Wirral. We loved the peace and space. We had two acres and after growing up with no greenery around us, it was a beautiful change.

Pauline kept her secretarial job until we were married, but then I insisted she gave it up because I didn't want to return from touring to find my wife not at home during the day.

We were all growing up and life was changing. Pauline and I became parents with the arrival of Yvette Louise on 30 October 1966. Sadly, with all my touring, I didn't get to see much of her growth in the first few years, though I came home as often as possible. Yvette was a great baby with no problems. She went on to take a strong interest in horse riding and show jumping and I enjoyed taking her round to the events with the big horse-box attached to the car. One of the best horses Yvette had was called Kelly's Golden Sovereign, which she kept until she found a boyfriend and got a car, and then it was goodbye horses! Yvette is engaged to be married in 1993.

Pauline and I eventually chose a holiday home in Anglesey and in the early days of Yvette's life we enjoyed many weekends there, I grew to love the place and although it was a hectic period for my career – tearing round the country for concerts or doing summer seasons in Blackpool or Great Yarmouth – I loved to retreat to Anglesey with my family, because of its calm. And I still do.

4

Farewell to a Friend

A New Stage

I love Liverpool. I'm very proud of it. It's like no other city in the world. 'Life goes on day after day/Hearts torn in every way,' I wrote in 'Ferry'. 'People they rush everywhere/Each with their own secret care.'

Writing a song that tried to capture part of the spirit of the Liverpudlian came easily to me. And it emphasised to me that unique spirit of the people who make up my home. I'm lucky to have two strong records ingrained into the Liverpool consciousness.

A few weeks after I'd recorded 'You'll Never Walk Alone' in 1963, it was sung by the crowd at Anfield. And through the years, Liverpool football club and I have become strongly linked because the song has been adopted as their anthem. It has a special, hymnal quality, equivalent perhaps to 'Abide With Me', such is the strength of feeling that runs through it. It's sung before the kick-off and intermittently through the matches at the Kop End of the Liverpool ground, by faithful supporters who find solidarity with its words; the Kop was named after Spion Kop in South Africa, where local men lost their lives in the Boer War.

'Walk Alone' was at number one on 22 November 1963, when President Kennedy was assassinated, and it's had a huge, warming impact on crowds in Liverpool and all round the world whenever I've sung it.

I became friends with the whole Liverpool team and they would sometimes come over to my house in Caldy for parties. To me they were the greatest team Liverpool ever had in that 1963–68 period, and we'd have some drinks together whenever their teetotal manager 'Shanks' wasn't looking. Ian St John, Tommy Smith, Ronnie Yates, Ian Callaghan, Tommy Lawrence, Chris Lawler and later Kevin Keegan became really good friends. The new team, with people like Mark Wright and Bruce Grobbelaar, are my mates now and I always try to keep a good contact with the team through all the changes.

It's strange that I should have become so closely associated with Liverpool football club, because originally I was an Everton supporter. My Uncle Gerard used to take me to see Everton, which the whole family supported . . . and because this produced no interesting disagreements over breakfast on Sunday mornings after the matches, I decided when I was about thirteen to support Liverpool. That way, at least we'd have something to discuss or, more accurately put, argue about.

When Liverpool FC's supporters adopted 'Walk Alone', it led to one of the best friendships of my life. I got a call from Bill Shankly, the club's genius manager. 'You're an inspiration for Liverpool football, my son,' he said to me. He developed into an exceptional friend and with his wife Nessie he came to dinner and told millions of jokes which had us roaring.

Shanks came down to Liverpool from Scotland, but he might as well have come from heaven as far as I was concerned. He was a Scotsman who never drank, swore very little and was a very hard case. He was a great winner – losing just didn't enter his mind – and he instilled this in the team of Liverpool to make it the world-beating institution that it still is. He transformed the club into the gods of football. It was one man's vision.

'I am a people's man, only the people matter,' he once said, and from my show-business perspective, I fully agreed with him – on that statement and on his whole philosophy.

During my visit to New York in 1964, when I was appearing on the 'Ed Sullivan Show', I was just starting my association with the team. As they were in the same city at that time, I had the pleasure of getting them a guest appearance on the programme, which was a tremendous boost for them. Shanks was over the moon.

'Gerry, my son, you're making us famous all over the worr-r-r-ld,' he rasped with that great Scottish burr.

He and Brian Epstein are two of the nicest people I've met, and the most influential. Brian because of his charisma and charm, Shankly because of his will to win and his lovely attitude to life. Nobody could beat that attitude. No wonder the team respected him as unrepeatable and no wonder he will be immortalised for generations.

I developed a passion for the club that continues to this day and became very friendly with several of the players, notably Mark Wright who lives close by me now and is a family friend. Whenever I go to see them play, which is as often as I can make it, a great wave of pride comes over me. It's just nice to have that association with the club.

Two of the most emotional moments in my life occurred through it all. When Shanks died and they put up the Shankly Gates at the entrance to the club in his memory, they asked me if I'd mind if they put over them the words 'You'll Never Walk Alone'. *Mind?* I said I'd physically do it myself if they let me. It's an honour, and I know Shanks would love that.

The other event surrounding Shanks was his memorial service. I was asked by his widow Nessie to sing at Liverpool Cathedral and when I went to the altar with my guitar to sing 'You'll Never Walk Alone', the congregation joined in. It was one of the most touching moments of my life; I could hear Shanks singing along with me, as well as 5,000 people standing outside the cathedral.

What is it exactly that makes Liverpool so different? If I had to go for one word, I'd say survival. Liverpool's heart is always trying to get over things, to put a brave face against adversity. Our heritage came from being a seaport, with many thousands of people coming into the city from all over the world, mixing with the locals in the pubs and clubs – and influencing us with their differences in humour, the arts and music.

We didn't have an industrial base in Liverpool: no steel, no coal, just cotton many years ago – but that's gone. Newcastle, Glasgow and Manchester are also hard cities that tend to turn out loads of comedians, but Liverpool has always leaned towards the artistic; and being a docks city, the outlook becomes more international.

It's not prosperous. People have to get by and make a gag about living on the edge of bankruptcy and getting over it. Years ago, when the docks were very active, we had all the ships bringing cotton into the city and those magnificent houses being built in the Parliament Street area during the seventeenth century. Since then, there hasn't been a lot.

Liverpool folk are sea gypsies; we all want to travel. There's a standing joke that to live in Liverpool you need to be a comedian. Sport, particularly boxing and football, provided a way out beyond the limits of Liverpool, and then in the late 1950s and 1960s, pop music came along and many of us grabbed it, realising that it was a route for a career beyond Liverpool – not because we didn't love our city, but because you had to go farther afield to extend and expand yourself in your chosen field. The list of Liverpudlian talents on the world stage in the entertainment and arts fields alone is gigantic. And I'm proud of that fact.

'Come on, let's get on with life' – that's an essential ingredient in the attitude of the natives. If there is a horrible disaster one day, in Liverpool the next day there will be forty-seven jokes about it. Sometimes they're sick, but that bouncing back helps people to survive. We don't mope about things. The feeling is more like 'Well, let's have a laugh about it, because you can't get back what's just happened.' Coventry and London and Liverpool, particularly being a seaport, got a hammering in the war, and there are millions of jokes still being traded about it in Liverpool. My upbringing was certainly on the basis of 'Don't let anything get you down too much.'

Going into the entertainment business, having that special Liverpool feeling has helped. I want to invite people to a party and keep them with me to enjoy it, because I'm having a great time and I don't want them to stand outside and miss it. Show business gives me the opportunity to lift people out of their low spots, inject a bit of brightness into their lives, make people forget their hassles. I like to keep people upright and entertained, and don't want to give them time to be miserable.

Writing in his autobiography, Brian Epstein recalled how 'amazed' he had been to find that nobody had approached me before him with an offer of management. He described me as 'one of the biggest stars in Liverpool with a smile as wide as he was short, a huge, generous personality and a fascinating voice full of melody and feeling'.

Brian went on to say:

I love watching Gerry at work – his communication with an audience, his winks and his nods and his feeling for humour and pathos. Off stage he is a robust and earthy character with an impressively salty vocabulary, but on stage he is the boy-next-door who would no more swear than miss an engagement.

Brian said that Princess Alexandra had twice requested my appearance at society balls, and he went on to predict a future for me in the wider sphere of show business. 'Gerry is no butterfly on the scene,' he wrote. 'He will be with us for a great many years because you cannot exhaust natural ability and because a pop singer who sends his first three discs to number one does not do it by accident.'

I only wish poor Brian had shown as much common sense about his own business as he showed about mine, the Beatles, Cilla's and others. By taking on too many artists, and getting too flamboyant in his thinking, he blew it. I told him so many times that he was taking on too many acts. The problem that arose from this was that his special touch as manager – and his determination to get the bookings correct – was lost. He took no notice of the warnings and it was the beginning of his downfall.

By the middle of 1966, Brian was in trouble. What he had told me about not being able to devote much time to my career had come true, but that was only the tip of his difficulties. He and the Beatles took a hammering in the States after John Lennon's statement that the group was 'more popular than Jesus', and Brian took the brunt of the attack when he went there to smooth things down before their tour.

When he returned to London, he looked ill. He had always enjoyed gambling, but then he got far too heavily into it at expensive places like Crockford's and the Clermont; he started losing heavily. He'd win £11,000 one night, and lose £15,000 the next.

In his autobiography, Brian had also written about me:

Away from his work, Gerry has been a wonderful friend to me. He is intelligent and kind and more than any of the other artistes he wants to demonstrate his friendship with presents. From him I've had gold cuff links, bracelet, tie pins and he remains the most outwardly grateful of all the people I manage.

All this was true, but it only increased my anger that Brian would not listen to my good advice. Although it was his money to lose, I warned him against the stupidity of his gambling. Once, I grabbed his cheque book off him to dissuade him from going out and blowing another few thousand pounds, but of course he would find ways round this.

Brian Epstein's personal life was a huge problem for him. He was a homosexual in the years when it was illegal and it caused him a lot of anguish. All of us managed by him knew about this and while it never interfered with our excellent business friendship with him, it worried him that he did not have a stable relationship.

I liked him very dearly and appreciated the good things he'd taught me about how to deal with people. He was a man with style and money. As a Catholic, I'd never met a Jew until I met Brian, and he came from a very successful Liverpool business family – they had *cars*! – that we thought was beyond our reach as rock 'n' roll kids. But he never made us feel inferior; he always urged me not to be aggressive to people simply because they'd disagreed with me, which was important advice to a natural fighter like me. Brian's beauty was that he gave all this advice casually. He was a great help to me in growing up. So when he needed a shoulder to cry on, I was always there. I think I was unique in getting phone calls from him at three in the morning: 'Gerry, I need to speak to you now, please.' I'd get out of bed and go and see him, and he'd often pour his heart out about his personal problems, how they worried him; he had the stupidity of a child at times.

It wasn't good to find Brian in such an agitated state so many times. The big problem was that he got involved with the 'rough trade' aspects of homosexuality and it worried him that this would one day rebound on him. He lived in fear of being found out.

I pointed out to him that if I had ignored *his* advice from the start, we would not be sitting there and the Beatles wouldn't have happened the way they did. 'We listened to *you* all the way, Brian. So now listen to *me*.' I said he should also level with all his artists about his private life; they'd still respect him. 'Come out and tell the truth, Brian. Don't keep it bottled up – there's no need for this worry,' I said to him. It wasn't that they didn't know, just that Brian swept it under the carpet from most of them. With me, he somehow felt he could open up. Those were different days for homosexuals and he felt the pressure.

'You're right, Gerry. I'm glad you came round. I needed that. I'm going to get some sleep now. Thank you.' Two nights later,

Brian would call again, in the same state. I told him not to worry, but I was dealing with a deeply troubled man.

Too much had happened too quickly for him. In four years he had built up this huge empire which was out of his control, he'd started dabbling in drugs and he was trying to keep his homosexuality secret.

Towards the end of his troubled year of 1966, Brian told me he was taking over as promoter of pop shows at the Saville Theatre in London's Shaftesbury Avenue. He always had an ambition to be a West End impresario and it was a wonderful idea to present the best of American and British pop at his own place. But I just knew he was not capable of pulling it off as well as running all his other projects.

'Brian, you're making a big mistake. It's daft,' I told him. He was investing a lot of his own money in the venture and I forecast, 'You're going to screw yourself for many, many thousands of pounds.'

I was one of the theatre's first bookings, playing alongside my old Hamburg buddy Fats Domino, and a newish group the Bee Gees, for six nights from 27 March 1967. I recently discovered my old 'running order' for this show: I opened with 'Dizzy Miss Lizzy', followed by 'I Like It', 'Hallelujah I Love Her So', Jerry Lee Lewis's oldie 'It'll Be Me', 'A Shot of Rhythm and Blues' on which I was joined vocally by brother Fred, 'Whole Lotta Shakin' Goin' On', 'You Win Again' (the old Hank Williams song), 'How Do You Do It?', 'Pretend' and 'You'll Never Walk Alone'.

In one way, Brian succeeded with the Saville Theatre. He presented some phenomenal talent: Chuck Berry, Bo Diddley, Jimi Hendrix, Ben E. King, Cream (with Eric Clapton), Lee Dorsey, Little Richard – it was a great artistic achievement. But as predicted by me and others, the Saville lost Epstein money and that depressed him still further. I think everyone in Brian's circle worried about him, but we all felt powerless about putting him back on the right track.

By an amazing coincidence, the Beatles and I were five miles apart on the weekend of 27 August 1967 when the news broke that made such a change to our lives. The Beatles had got into meditation with the Maharishi Mahesh Yogi; I wasn't in the least bit interested in all that, and it didn't register that they were only a few miles away until I arrived at Anglesey.

There was no phone at my Anglesey home, and a farmer came to say there was a Norman Cowan on his phone calling from London for me. Strange; I knew him as Brian Epstein's doctor. The farmer said the news was bad: Brian was dead. I refused to believe it. As I went to the phone, I contradicted him. I said Brian must be sick. 'Hi, Norman,' I said. 'I hope you're not gonna tell me what this friend of mine here just said.' It was true. I felt empty. We all saw it coming, but the reality was shocking.

Brian had died accidentally, the inquest decided later, from a combination of alcohol and sleeping pills. The news blew us all apart; everyone who had made it out of Liverpool owed so much to him and, despite all his difficulties, we loved him. Losing him was bad enough; I felt even more sorry for his family. Only six weeks earlier, his father Harry had died and we were all at Liverpool Jewish Cemetery with Queenie and her younger son Clive. Now we were back to bury Brian. I don't know how she got through.

I'm often asked what would have happened if Brian Epstein had lived. For myself, I'm pretty sure he would not have continued to manage me. I wanted to move into the West End theatre, and I was confident enough to take control of the pattern of my own career; you progress in life or you stand still, and I was ambitious. I'd probably have asked him to remain in an advisory position. I valued him and would not have forgotten what he'd done for us. Somebody had to go and find a George Martin, somebody had to talk to people for us, somebody had to tell us how to shape up, and Brian was marvellous at that period in our lives. But he, too, constantly wanted change.

I don't think the Beatles would have stayed together, either.

They'd been together successfully for about seven years. They were getting fed up with touring together and that's not to criticise any of them. John and Paul were becoming childish and stupid towards each other when they drifted apart. You can't be together in the same band for all that time without getting restless. You grow up and make money, which changes a lot of outlooks. They'd have split, anyway.

It's impossible to say which way Brian would have gone. He loved the theatre, so maybe that would have been his destiny had he lived. I count myself lucky to have met him and gained from him; I just wish that he'd survived longer so that I could have got to know him a lot better. He was a great man who crammed a lot into a short life, and made a lot of people happy.

After Brian's death, I was at sea, like all of us who knew him. He'd steered us through a very heady period and though I had some concerts to get on with, the future was uncertain. I got lucky. A phone call from Bernie Lee at NEMS, Brian's management company, told me that after two years of acting in the show, Joe Brown was coming out of a West End musical, *Charlie Girl*, and would I like to audition for the part? I said, 'I'd love to.'

So began one of the happiest experiences of my life. I listened to the soundtrack album, went down to the Adelphi Theatre to sing a couple of the songs on stage – and got the role of Joe Studholme, playing opposite Anna Neagle as Lady Hadwell, and Derek Nimmo, the Liverpudlian actor. Not only was I lucky in getting a West End break in the theatre, but with the charming Dame Anna and Derek Nimmo I had the best teachers anyone could have wished for. They came in themselves to rehearse with me rather than sending in understudies, and they were wonderfully inspirational and welcoming.

I'd had to disband the Pacemakers, which was sad, but I felt we'd had our best run with that line-up anyway. We'd had five years of success and, though we were still popular, there was nothing happening on the record front and I wanted progress in my career. Pauline remembers that, as far back as she can remember, I'd been saying my ambition was to appear on a West End stage.

I kept watching Tommy Steele and thought he had made a great transformation from singing songs like 'Singing the Blues' into stage musicals. That was the route I fancied too, and Brian Epstein had repeatedly told me, 'You will one day appear on the stage.' I called him a lying git, because it was beyond my wildest dreams.

We sold the house in Caldy and rented one in Hanger Lane, Ealing, but this was a very weird experience. I soon became convinced that the place was haunted. Paintings would fall off the walls, sliding mirrors would go into the walls and reveal closets. We heard strange noises coming from the sun lounge and Pauline would make me go and see who it was. I remember going to the bottom of the stairs shouting, 'If you're there, I'm coming up, so you'd better run!' – while all the time I was frightened to death. We had a nanny living with us, an Irish girl called Madeline, who used to say, 'Gerry, I can hear gargling noises in the night!' This was a kind of choking sound. The whole place put us all on edge.

After about six months there I was in the bank one day and met our postman. 'Hi, Gerry,' he said. 'What do you think of Hanger Lane?' I said it was fine. 'What do you think of the house?' he said. I said it wasn't bad and why did he ask? 'Have you heard the story about that place?' he said. He went on to tell me that a year before we moved in, a nanny had been murdered there in particularly gruesome circumstances. I didn't dare tell Pauline at that time, but started looking for a new home. As well as wanting to get away from Ealing, it was time to settle into something more permanent. Jimmy Tarbuck tipped me off that Tom Jones was wanting to sell his nice house in Sunbury-on-Thames.

I had a very good friendship with Tom that dated back to just before he became famous. We had topped the bill when he was well down it, with his band the Squires. I'd always go and see other acts perform from the wings, and during one tour, when Tom came off, he asked me what I thought. I said, 'The voice is great but stop all that *moving*! It's old hat, it's crap.' Of course, Tom's body movements later became one of the strongest and sexiest parts of his stage act. Eventually, when Tom had his huge hit with 'It's Not Unusual', we were on a radio show in London together. I heard his voice booming out at me, 'Gerry, the voice is nice, but you'd better start some bloody *moving*, boyo!'

So it was good to be buying the boyo's house, and starting the enjoyable residency in *Charlie Girl*. David Heneker and John Taylor, who wrote the music, even wrote a song specially for my arrival: it was called 'Liverpool'; Derek Nimmo and I sang it, and it proved very popular with the audience. So we released it on record. The show was light and easy – about people in a stately home – and just what audiences wanted for a carefree night out.

Apart from working on stage with some of the best professionals in the theatre, I loved the friendships that developed inside *Charlie Girl*. Anna Neagle, such a delightful lady of old-fashioned charm, called me 'My little Gerry'. Appearing in a play was a different experience for me: there was a script to learn and stick to. There was no 'flying by the seat of your pants', as we all did in pop groups. No knocking jokes to and fro with the audience. But I loved it and seemed to do well with the crowds from the start. I always think that if you *look* like you're having a ball, it rubs off, and I sure enjoyed every moment of the work.

There was no way I was going to fail on the stage after all those years of waiting for it. I could see the critics lining up with 'obituaries' for me, saying a pop star had failed to make the switch. I could hear them saying, 'Let's see a pop star die!' No way was I going to die in the West End, and with the help of Dame Anna and Derek Nimmo, two of the greatest people I met in my life, I was able to rehearse thoroughly and learn the part. So I worked bloody hard and won!

My dresser was Derek Harknett. He was an experienced wardrobe master and, as always with people I work with, I made a friend of him quickly. For a long time, though, he couldn't understand the Liverpool nutter who changed all the rules he'd come to live by in the theatre! In particular, he could not get to grips with my casual way with people. For example, he had to dress me several times in the course of each show, and after each change he'd say, 'I'll be outside if you want me.'

I said, 'Where are you going? Have I offended you or something?'

He explained that the procedure for wardrobe assistants like him was to do the job and then leave the actor alone, as a courtesy. I didn't go for that.

'Sit down. We're together in this. Relax and have a drink,' I told him. He became part of it all and thoroughly enjoyed meeting my friends, taking them to and from their seats and into my dressing room: people like Bill Shankly, John Lennon, Ringo Starr and Paul McCartney. There was, most nights, quite a procession.

Derek Harknett remembers that the whole cast referred to my room as 'the Green Room', meaning the hospitality room in theatre language, because it was so full of visitors.

'The cast often went from the stage to Gerry's room; and he loved it because he loved company all the time,' Derek says.

Before long Derek and I were getting on like pals and he had fun with my pranks and humour. He remembers the nights when I panicked him into thinking I would never be ready in time for my cue to go on stage:

Once I had Gerry dressed ready to go on for a really vital entrance, a scene with Anna Neagle, and if he didn't appear it would be curtains for all of us. I was just about to say, 'You'd better get out there now,' when Gerry said, 'I've got to go to the toilet.' He began to take his trousers down to prove that he meant it.

He went into the toilet and bolted the door. I hammered

on it, begging him to come out. I was in my biggest panic ever. I rushed out to get the stage manager, and told him Gerry was sick; at least he could then hold Anna back. I was practically in tears. The stage manager looked horrified and then said, 'What are you talking about? There's Gerry *on stage* with Anna.' It transpired that he'd gone into the toilet to give me a scare and had watched me going berserk at the stage manager while he calmly walked on stage in time. When he came off, I was a shaken wreck and Gerry had to beat his hands on the dressing table to stop himself from yelling with laughter.

'Sorry, Degs!' he said. 'I just couldn't help it. You should have just seen yourself!' When I recovered from the shock I laughed just as much.

There was an especially funny episode when Anna Neagle went down with pneumonia and a delightful lady, Evelyn Laye, came in to deputise for her. She acted so magnificently that, at the end of her first night, the audience stood to applaud her and a girl came on to present her with a beautiful bouquet of flowers. We all took a bow and as she moved forward the rest of the cast moved back and the curtain, thankfully made of cloth, came down; it hit her on the head and knocked her down. 'Boo' Laye, as we affectionately nicknamed her, was now on the floor with her head and her flowers out at the front of the house and her legs and skirt at the back!

Derek Nimmo looked at me and said, 'Oh God, what do we do?' We decided to get hold of her feet and pull her from under the curtain. Derek got hold of one leg, I got the other, and as we pulled her out she was waving to the audience! What a professional she was! As we pulled her back, the whole cast was standing with straight faces – but when she stood up and pulled herself together, she looked at us all and declared, 'You may now smile!'

On another occasion, I asked Derek to phone Whitehall police and ask them what time I had to appear to one of their dances. Derek remembers:

> He sat at his dressing table and got me in such a state and a muddle that I ended up by asking the lady who answered my call if she knew anybody who knew anything about the policemen's balls, and if not could she put me through to somebody who did. Through this, Gerry was laughing so much I had to hang up. Eventually, after the show, the police collected him and Pauline in one of their cars with all sirens blaring through the streets.

I don't like drinking alone and this caused another amusing scene with Derek backstage. I kept asking him to join me in a glass of whisky but he was under medical orders to abstain. So for many months, unknown to me, he pretended to be drinking by adding about an inch of Guinness to a glass of water, which made it look like whisky. I thought I had a drinking partner in those dressing-room moments – until one day, I came off stage and accidentally took a gulp out of his glass.

'Good God, Degs, this is bloody horrible,' I said, 'what is it?' I was amazed that he'd conned me for so long, and also that he'd been drinking such a vile concoction.

When John and Ringo, with their wives at the time, Cynthia and Maureen, came to see the show, Derek steered them to my dressing room for the interval. Before I arrived, John was playing with my guitar, which worried Derek; and when John then poured himself a whole tumbler full of whisky from my usual bottle, Derek panicked because he didn't want me to return to an empty bottle of Bell's.

The general tension really got to Derek and he threatened to leave me every few weeks, but he never meant it; we had a great friendship. He used to come and babysit with Yvette, who was then two years old, and stay the night with us. He could never get over the fact that I'd get up next morning, cook him breakfast and then drive him to the theatre. He seemed to

105

think 'stars' were all stand-offish, but I've never felt any distance from someone I'm working with. It's more fun, more human, that way.

Only one thing saddened me about *Charlie Girl* – that Brian Epstein hadn't lived to see me on that stage. It would have been pure magic for him to see one of his wishes and predictions come true. Pauline and I often said how much we wished he hadn't died when he did. A year after his death, three of his acts had achieved precisely what he had said they would: the Beatles were bigger than Elvis; I had made it to the West End for a musical; and Cilla was on her way to becoming a very successful TV personality. I could never see Brian living to a ripe old age, but I hope he got plenty of pleasure from putting a lot of us on the path to success.

Charlie Girl was a happy hit with the audiences, but the critics slagged it. Naturally, this meant it was a glorious success and ran for nearly six years. It was an old-fashioned family show and I shall always consider it, and the people I met through it, to be among the real highlights of my life and career. Beautiful people, nice family atmosphere. And I'd made the West End stage!

When *Charlie Girl* reached its natural end, I went into another musical. *Pull Both Ends* was a comedy set in a Christmas cracker factory, and opened in Manchester before moving to the Piccadilly Theatre in London. The Young Generation dance team were in it and although the show was fun, it had financial problems early on. We all took cuts in wages to help it along but the writing was on the wall and it struggled along for eighteen months before closing.

This at least gave me the impetus to do something I'd wanted to do throughout the years I'd been in theatre – move back up north. I just didn't like London. It was too busy. I loved the genuine Londoners I met, but it was so cosmopolitan that Pauline and I didn't meet many of what I'd call 'real people'. Most of them were from all over the place, and since I was busy working every day and night, I could never consider London home.

Deep down, I always intended returning to Merseyside after finishing 'the job' in London. I wanted my roots back.

Pauline didn't mind the South as much as I did. The house at Sunbury was very comfortable, but the moment I bottled out was when it was getting close to the time for Yvette to start school at the age of five. I knew that once she began, we wouldn't be able to move for a long time. One day I walked in the house and said, 'Come on, start packing, we're moving.'

Pauline, taken aback by the speed of it, said, 'What *are* you doing?'

I said simply, 'We're going home.'

There was another aspect to all this. I didn't want to join the show-business clique, the 'rat pack' that exists in London. Nothing wrong with it if you like it, but my show business consists of entertaining on the stage. I've never been comfortable with the 'dahling' and 'lovey dovey' aspects of showbiz.

When I'm off duty and at a friend's house, I don't need to show off by standing on the table singing 'Ferry' or 'Walk Alone'. But so many of these people were comics who felt they had to amuse you with half a dozen gags before dinner. I like to relax and get away from show business when I'm not working, and there was a hard core of showbiz folk who never seemed to want to get off stage and behave normally. It was difficult not to get sucked into their world; if we turned down all the invitations, we'd have been considered unfriendly.

As Pauline says, remembering that part of our lives:

So often, on Gerry's luxurious night off, we'd just want to sit in front of the television after a nice dinner with a bottle of wine. And as we did, the phone would ring with someone saying something like, 'It's so-and-so's opening night at the Talk of the Town or wherever ... you must come. You *should be there*.' There was a lot of 'being seen' in all this, and Gerry disliked that cliquey side of it.

I couldn't wait to return 'home'. We bought a house on the

Wirral and I breathed a huge sigh of relief. The London experience was something I'm glad I didn't miss. But I decided then, in 1971, that I'd always want to live in or near Liverpool. I probably inherited the strength of that feeling from my parents, who still live in the Dingle; the house in which I was raised was the last one in Menzies Street to be demolished to make way for a new development, but Mum and Dad lived there till the end ... and even then moved to one very close to it.

5

The Pendulum Swings

Walking Alone

I faced a tough time after leaving the theatre. Even though I'd not been playing music for nearly four years, my yearning for it was still strong and I decided I wanted to return to my roots in pop, just as I had in returning to live in Liverpool.

I've always been an 'up' person by nature. Luckily, I've not had any truly bad experiences, but when I have had difficulties I've always battled against them, thought positively and tried to analyse what happened. It's partly the Liverpool in me which says: Well, what can be done about this bad news? Answer: Very little, usually. So I pull myself into a frame of mind that is not depressed. I bounce back. My continual bounce drives Pauline mental at times.

'I wish you'd take things more seriously,' she says. My reply is that I don't want to take seriously things that are going to bring me down.

I decided to re-form the Pacemakers. It wasn't a very smooth journey back; the musical climate in those early 1970s was changing into what people called 'meaningful rock', difficult for me as my career had been launched when singles, and the personality of the artist, were what counted.

Back in the Sixties when I told Brian Epstein I expected the good times to last for me for about five years, I had no idea what the future held. After Brian's death and my years on the West End stage, my desire to pick up the reins of my career as a travelling musician was hampered a little by the musical mood of the early Seventies. All those heavy rock bands like Led Zeppelin and Yes and heavy metal like Black Sabbath suddenly made the 1960s music unfashionable. The philosophy was entirely different. We called it pop; we were 'groups'. The 1970s acts called it rock – and they were 'bands'.

A few people in the business tried to dissuade me, telling me my sound was 'old hat', but determination is one of my strongest points.

Some friends said to me, 'You'll never get back.' The battler in me responded to this. I didn't like being told I was a has-been, so I decided without any doubt that I'd prove them all wrong. I went out into the clubs with just a pianist until I found musicians; I really needed this experience as I hadn't played for about three years.

It was a little like what Paul McCartney did at that time: the Beatles had just split up and Macca's first instincts were to form a new band, Wings, and get out and tour. That's the life he enjoyed best, and he lost no time in doing it again in small halls around Britain. When I saw him doing this, I thought, 'Good lad. Just what you should be doing.' It wasn't for money, but to entertain people. That's how it all began for all of us.

I hadn't lost confidence, but after all that time following a script on stage, with no ad-libbing, I'd forgotten what it was like to talk to people. I wanted that freedom back. I missed it, and I realised I had been restricted in the West End theatre. (Derek Nimmo and I had got away with a bit of ad-libbing, but mostly, of course, you have to stick to the script.)

Starting back, I went in at the bottom. I played a lot of dreadful venues, got paid nothing, but 'found myself' again through sheer hard graft. Financially it was not easy, but psychologically the challenge was just what I needed. This was evidence of the sea gypsy in me again, the Liverpool traveller, that couldn't stand still. From playing some horrendous gigs like the discos, I gradually worked back to the theatres and concert halls.

I didn't believe in beating about the bush. I was actively looking for work. I guessed it might be tough re-establishing myself, so I'd ring up clubs and say, 'Are you empty tonight?' If they were, I'd say we were going down to play because it would attract an audience into the club who would spend money on drinks. Some of the club managers thought I was kidding – they couldn't believe we wanted to do this for small money, but I thought it was vital to spread the word. It was obvious to me the public was there; they all knew my name, which was a great advantage.

As I began touring again, I felt the buzz. I gradually hired musicians and went through a few changes until I came to the right combination. It was uphill, but in spite of the awful places and hard audiences, we never lost the fight. Luckily, we had the hit records on our side; people still remembered them, so it wasn't as hard for us as it was for many bands returning to the road. Thank God it worked.

Whatever branch of show business we are in, we all need two ingredients extra to talent: good management and a stroke of luck. Mine came together when, in the autumn of 1972, I appeared for a week at a venue in Bradford called the Talk of Yorkshire. This was nine years after my run of hits in 1963, so according to my old calculations I was on borrowed time.

But the compère at the Talk of Yorkshire was Derek Franks, who was gradually changing his career pattern from singing middle-of-the-road songs in the clubs to become a manager and an agent.

In those days, I preferred to go to most of my appearances by train rather than drive. Partly because of this, with Derek driving me, we became quite friendly, even playing tennis a few times during the period (or, more accurately, I played tennis while Derek attempted to hit the ball back).

About six months later, in February 1973, I was appearing at the famous Batley Variety Club. By then, Derek had stopped touring and was resident compère over at the Talk of Yorkshire. He came to see me at Batley.

I was staying at the Black Horse, a pub at Clifton, about four miles away. I got a taxi back there after every show; but naturally Derek offered to give me a lift and when we arrived he came in for a drink.

It was the sort of place where the landlord went to bed and left you to help yourself from the bar and put it on your bill next day. So naturally, after a few hours, Derek and I were in a suitably relaxed state – but the conversation was still flowing. Derek takes up the story:

It came round to me saying to Gerry, 'Where are you working next week?'

'Oh, I don't know,' he said.

'The week after?' I asked him.

'I don't really know.'

I didn't say anything to him about it, but I got the strong impression that he didn't have much work at the time.

I don't think he was down in the dumps, but I felt he was simply accepting what he regarded as the inevitable: that he'd go round and do the odd week here and there, a pantomime and a summer season. I also got the impression he felt that he'd had a good innings, that perhaps the Sixties bubble had burst and he was now on his way out. In his show, I was surprised to see he was calling himself Gerry Marsden and the New Pacemakers, and doing a comedy routine with the audience with the song 'Old Macdonald had a Farm', quite strange and very unusual for a pop star.

112

As the night wore on until three o'clock in the morning, Derek told me he was setting up his own agency – and he declared that he could get me some good bookings. I said, 'Fine.' He added that if by eleven o'clock next morning he phoned me with seven consecutive weeks' work, I was to sign a management contract with him. I replied, 'OK, I'll do that.'

Derek remembers:

At 10.30 next morning I rang him and told him I'd got him nine weeks' work. I sent him a management contract which I had drawn up by solicitors. Twenty years later, he hasn't signed it or sent it back, but I'm still his manager.

I think Derek and I know that we were both lucky: I got just what I needed at that time, a good manager, and he got a major attraction just as he was beginning his agency. He seemed to have an inkling that I could be part of the return of artists from the Sixties, and he has been proved correct; it was certainly unfashionable at that time, but the pendulum has swung and Derek positioned me, in a business sense, to be able to take full advantage of it.

The first argument we had was about our name. After the West End theatre appearances, I'd appeared simply as Gerry Marsden, but that was because I had a pianist and no band. When I added piano, bass and drums, I had to call it something and the old name didn't sound true, so I called it 'New . . .'

Derek said, 'We can't continue to call it that.'

I said, 'Of course we can. In fact, we've got to. It's not the old band.'

But Derek insisted that a revised line-up didn't mean we should change what was basically my strongest point of identity, my trademark name. I was stubborn, of course, but over a period of twelve months, he did it gradually. First he called me Gerry Marsden and the Pacemakers in bookings and then he just dropped 'Marsden'.

'As soon as I dropped the Marsden,' Derek says, 'the good

work flooded in. Because everybody recognised the fact that Gerry and the Pacemakers were the ones who had all those hits.'

The policy Derek adopted to get me re-established was to book me into the smaller venues, to spread my name and also to rebuild my confidence a little. This was helped by the fact that I was packing in the crowds to capacity. Derek recalls:

> He wasn't quite sure where he was going. The Sixties were not the flavour of the month or year, and don't forget that Gerry had stopped having hits back in 1965. With all the new breed of singer-songwriters, Gerry couldn't compete with them with his pretty little hits like 'How Do You Do It?' and 'I Like It'.

As an example of how he slowly built me up: the first engagement he booked for me in 1973 was for six nights at the Park Hall in Charnock Richard, Lancashire. This was a cabaret room in a medium-sized hotel at the time. For those six nights I received £850. I was quite happy with this: the band's wages in those days were about £250 in total for the week.

We haven't played that venue since. It's now a big hotel with a large function suite and I'm booked there for two nights on 26 and 27 November 1993 – exactly twenty years since my first and last appearance there – but this time for a fee of £7000.

Derek says now:

> I worked very hard in getting him work, but I was convinced I could get him plenty of it for two simple reasons. One, he was good, and two, he had the added advantage of having an established name. I'd seen a lot of the Sixties bands that were absolute crap. Gerry's was a good act and I followed the old show-business rule that a good act should be able to be in regular work.

Also, he'd adapted his show quite cleverly to the cabaret

market in which he was working, with routines like 'Old Macdonald's Farm'. Now, in 1993, he's adapted his show to the concert market. He is an entertainer, not merely a rock 'n' roller, and he's quite capable of changing for the public's demands. So what I saw back in the early Seventies was someone with a very strong future, and it was sacrilege to hear that he was not facing a full diary of engagements.

I took Gerry to work in some really grotty places to start with, just to get his name going again. It was a four-to-five-year project. I discussed everything with him, with questions like 'Where exactly do you want to work?' Gerry said he'd work anywhere. There was (and still is) a side to him that's a workaholic; he loves to be on the road, touring, and particularly enjoys the moments on stage . . . but there's always been, also, a part of him that enjoys being at home, pottering in the garden. For example, he likes to think he's a joiner.

I astounded Derek with one of my examples of 'woodwork'. In the 1960s, John Lennon and I were presented with specially made guitars by the Rickenbacker company, because they knew how much we admired the model. Only two of this particular design were made and I'd kept mine proudly for about fifteen years. Then, just before I was going off on a tour of Australia and New Zealand, Derek said to me, 'You'd better make sure you get some new flight cases for those guitars of yours, because the ones you've got are battered and they'll fall to pieces on the plane.'

I replied, 'I'll make one specially for the Rickenbacker.'

So I built this case for my priceless guitar of sentimental value, and then, the day before I was due to fly to Australia, I went to put the instrument in my carefully constructed new wooden case . . . and, of course, the case was too small. Impulsively, I sawed the neck of the guitar off. With any guitar, this would be considered an outrageous act, but this Rickenbacker was like a rare gem. It was custom-made and had a unique, beautifully shaped neck. I didn't realise the enormity of what I was doing until the deed had been done. Then I phoned Derek and told him.

'You have done *what?*' he asked, staggered. He couldn't believe it. I knew, then, the extent of the damage in every sense. The Rickenbacker couldn't be the same again, so I took it on tour with me and traded it in in New Zealand for a different guitar. So someone, somewhere, has a guitar with quite a history: one of only two in the world, but with its neck sawn off, a perfect example of my ham-fistedness.

He works me hard, but Derek and I have some tremendous laughs. We were doing a week in Bournemouth in 1975 and he had bought a new Volvo which he was boasting would 'go anywhere, do anything', so we decided to take it on the beach and sit and read the newspapers while facing the sea. As we sat idling the hours away, I saw the tide coming in and said several times to Derek, 'We'd better go pretty soon.'

His answer was always the same: 'Don't worry, it's a Volvo. These cars go anywhere, do anything.' Even when the tide neared the front of the car, he didn't worry. He put it into reverse and expected it to drive off. But it wouldn't.

'Get out and push, quick,' he said to me.

I went to the front and started pushing, but the car was on pebbles – and as Derek put it into reverse, the wheels started spinning and loads of pebbles flew into the air. Some hit me, knocking me flying, and there I was, sprawled on my back, in sea water on Bournemouth beach, while Derek laughed as the car successfully pulled away.

'The sight of you standing on that beach getting pebbles all over you was amazing, Gerry,' he said to me as I climbed back into the car. I believe I said something to him about going forth and multiplying.

I love boats and water ski-ing and one day in 1974 I was skiing in Corfu. A friend and I decided to swank in front of the camera, since Pauline had the video going. I would go under his boat and he would go over mine and we would cross. As I turned to wave to the camera I heard a voice shouting out to warn me:

A happy day. Pauline and me with the guvnor, Brian Epstein, who's saying, 'You wouldn't listen to me, son, but never mind.' I think we've proved we were right.

With Pauline and a very small Yvette Louise in Caldy.

'Pass me the hammer, Pauline, I can fix it!'

With the lovely Veronica Page in *Charlie Girl*, 1969.

Dinner after a *Charlie Girl* performance with Derek Nimmo and my dear friend, the boxer Alan Rudkin, who stopped me boxing and turned me towards showbiz. He's here with his friend Max.

Yes, it's me, second from the left, in my second musical, *Pull Both Ends*. What do you think of the gear, folks?

With Frankie Vaughan, meeting the Queen at the opening of the new Mersey Tunnel. Her Majesty is obviously dazzled by my bright white teeth.

Prince Charles and Liverpool Radio City chairman Ken Medlock at a carol service for Radio City. I wonder who stuck a silly sign on Prince Charles's back?

Gerry and the Pacemakers with Mike and Bernie Winters and friends in Miami in the late 1970s.

Twiggy and me; she came on the ferry to do a television show with me for the States. Twiggy is a lovely lady and I'll tell you, she's not a twig now!

Joe Brown of Bruvvers fame, Freddie Garrity of Freddie and the Dreamers and Reg Presley of the Troggs, together with Gerry Marsden. We were all appearing in an 'Unforgettable Nostalgia' concert in Croydon.

Above: 'I'm not nervous. I always shake like this!' On stage at Wembley Stadium at Cliff Richard's concert 'The Event'.

Right: With Cliff Richard at 'The Event'.

Peter Noone (once Herman of Hermits fame), me and Freddie Garrity doing a show for Peter's American television programme.

With the new Pacemakers, Andy Cairns, Kevin Jackson and Sean Fitzpatrick, who are saying, 'Hey, boss, you're definitely getting fatter!'

The happy family: Yvette, Vicky, Pauline and me. Love them to death!

Any old iron! At home, framed by the various awards I've collected over the years.

The ferry that crossed the Mersey for the last time. The *Royal Iris* was taken out of her dock in Liverpool and put to rest in Birkenhead in 1992. Have a nice rest, Iris, one of our most famous Liverpool names.

'Gerry, look out!' I thought my pal was heading to go under my boat, while he thought I was going under his. As I spun round, the ski rope missed my head by about a quarter of an inch. Had it connected, it would have been the first time decapitation had been on a home video. Luckily, I survived that disaster.

I'm very fond of my jet ski and a couple of years ago another near-disaster came upon me. My brother-in-law Peter Behan was on the beach at Anglesey as I started to travel very fast to show him how I could spin it round with skill. But at one moment I realised I was too near the beach, so I stuck the accelerator down hard – and I went straight over the handlebars, did three somersaults and landed on my back in the water. As he video-recorded the incident, I think Peter was highly impressed with my acrobatics more than with my jet ski-ing.

I go scuba diving, too, and once I got stuck down a cave, teaching me the lesson that we all know and that every book tells you – we should never dive alone. But I did, off Anglesey, where I often do this, and on this occasion my tanks got stuck in a crevice. I put my foot in the roof of the crevice to push my tanks off me, and as I pulled the tanks free my foot became jammed. So now I'm upside down in a cave, holding the lungs in front of me, with my foot jammed. I thought, 'This is the end!' Luckily, I pulled on my foot, taking the skin off my ankles and beyond, and managed to get the lungs back on. But it proved the point: you can *walk alone*, but never dive alone!

Another near-disaster with the water occurred when I took my younger daughter Vicky and her friends for a day's boating and picnicking on the River Weaver near Chester. As we pulled up alongside a field for the picnic, I warned the kids, 'One thing you must not do is walk near the mooring ropes, because if you trip over them, you're in the river.' They were playing around quite happily and eventually, as we finished eating and were packing everything back into the boat, I was shouting to them and I then tripped on the mooring ropes – and went straight into the river, carrying the picnic table with me! They all said, 'Good old Uncle Gerry, great show.' They always win!

On another occasion when we were on the boat we were going under a bridge, my brother-in-law Peter was in the bow and he said as we approached it, 'Gerry, I think the boat's too big to go under a bridge.'

I said, 'No problems, Peter, I was up here the other day and there was no difficulty at all.'

We chugged along and suddenly I got a call from Peter; as I turned round I saw that his head had cleared the bridge by about an inch and we'd nearly lost the top off the boat. What had happened was that the water had risen by a foot since my last visit. Luckily, full reverse thrust saved us, so I didn't rip the top off the boat.

Years earlier, when Yvette was fourteen, we were on the canal in Shropshire and a friend, Michael, was driving the boat and I was on the edge. I was showing I could do handstands on the side of the boat. Yvette said, 'Dad, you're going to fall in,' but I continued. As I went for my final handstand, sure enough I lost my balance and went straight into the water – and all she heard was me shouting, 'Shit' as I grabbed hold of my sunglasses and car keys which were hooked on to my pocket. Instead of putting the boat into reverse, Michael threw the lever forward and the boat went down the canal. I was left swimming behind it as fast as I could, fully dressed, completely knackered, and then suddenly my knee hit the bottom of the canal, whereupon I realised the water was all of three feet deep. I could have walked a lot faster!

I couldn't have someone representing me as manager whom I didn't relate to away from work. I get on so well with Derek that he probably knows more about me than I do. For the first seven years that he managed me he came to every show; then, when he got married in 1979 to Debra, I was his best man. I took the job extremely seriously, putting him to bed at the Hilton Hotel in Leeds the night before the wedding and instructing the whole hotel staff not to meet any requests by him for room service. As Derek and anyone who knows me will confirm, I have a strong practical joker inside me, but when events call for seriousness I can handle that, too.

My manager is pretty observant about my little idiosyncrasies. He points out that I have a 'thing' about chemists, a compulsion to go into them all round the world and spend a fortune on medicaments. Not for myself, because I'm not a hypochondriac, but for a strange reason: I like to be prepared for other people, particularly those around me, so if someone complains of a shoulder ache or whatever, I can say, 'Hold on, I have something for that.' I guess it's the part of me that wants to please.

'He'll give you anything you ask for,' Derek says, 'as long as it's not money. But when you're with him you don't spend. We were in Australia in the autumn of 1992 and Gerry said to me before we went out for a Chinese meal with a friend, "Make sure he pays because he hasn't paid all week." When the bill came, I said we should split it three ways, but within seconds, Gerry was up and had quietly paid it without anyone realising it. That's always the case.'

On the other side of the coin, I'm definitely keen to be paid for my work.

'If Gerry doesn't get paid at or before a show, World War Three will start!' says my manager. I can spend like it's going out of fashion, and the more I earn the more I spend so the more I work; it's a cycle.

People's fascination with the Sixties and its music has finally worked in my favour. By the late Seventies, the newer bands had made their impact, but it was then timely for those of us who had always had something to offer to reclaim our popularity. Ears were re-opening to the lively music of yesteryear and there was recognition that perhaps what the Beatles and Gerry and the Pacemakers began had some lasting value.

Where are the old Pacemakers now? It's a question I'm often asked nostalgically as I tour the world. Les Chadwick, my former bass guitarist, now lives in New South Wales, Australia, where he operates an employment agency and I see him on my visits there. Les Maguire, the pianist, changed careers dramatically and became a naval officer stationed in Scotland, though he and his wife have a house on Merseyside. His ship was active during the Gulf War. My brother Fred, our drummer, is in business in Liverpool, where he still lives.

The band which I had when Derek Franks became my manager was good, but I felt it was time to change the line-up after three years. Departures from my bands have usually been amicable – I don't like to end an association with any musician with a bad feeling.

It was in the late 1970s that the Sixties Revival concert tours began to gain popularity. In 1979, I went on my first, the 'Liverpool Explosion' tour of Britain, along with the Swinging Blue Jeans, Tommy Bruce, Dave Berry and Wayne Fontana and the Mindbenders. Derek Franks was the compère. We had a load of laughs as old mates would; and in the years since then I've joined other old friends like Billy J. Kramer, the Troggs, Herman's Hermits and Freddie and the Dreamers on hundreds of revival shows from London to New York. We had a particularly successful tour with two American friends and great artists, Bobby Vee and Tommy Roe, all round Britain in 1992, and 1993 brings a three-month 'Solid Gold Sixties' tour with me, the Searchers and Billy J. This is a thirtieth anniversary tour for some of us who broke through in 1963 and we're all going to have a great time together.

During one of these 'revival tour' shows in 1986, I was playing with Billy J. Kramer and Freddie and the Dreamers at Madison Square Garden, New York, and, as usual, the crowd was magnificent. As I took the bow at the end of the show, they all screamed and applauded and then, as I ran off to the left to go down the steps, I missed the steps (like in a scene from the cartoons where your feet are still in the air) and landed on top of a policeman. This smashed him to the floor. He staggered up, I established that he was OK and he said, 'I'm all right, Gerry, get back on that stage.' Running back, I was so pleased to have survived that little episode, that I got my guitar on, ran backwards a few steps and tripped over the monitor speaker. I finished on my back. I was so embarrassed that I stayed on the floor until the spotlight went on to the pianist for his solo spot. Then I got up and started singing.

My enthusiasm for practical jokes has driven many people mad, particularly my manager. I also try his patience in other ways. I've phoned him at two in the morning with a little problem that has occurred to me and which I think he should solve. After giving him what he describes as 'verbal abuse', I'll hang up and forget about it. Sometimes, Derek has zoomed over to see me very quickly after one of my outpourings, and I'll be amazed to see him.

'What are you doing here?' I've said in the past.

'I've come to sort out this bloody problem,' he says.

'What problem? Oh, I've forgotten about that now. Have a drink.' The verbal abuse is my way of letting off steam to whoever will listen, and once I've done that, my temper subsides.

The biggest shows I did, in terms of audiences, were with my old friend Cliff Richard, whose 'The Event' concerts at Wembley Stadium on 16 and 17 June 1989 were in front of 72,000 people each day. These shows spanned Cliff's entire career, and Gerry and the Pacemakers and the Searchers were representing the Sixties. Cliff came on at the end and sang 'You'll Never Walk Alone' with me. I loved the size of the crowds and the atmosphere of Wembley.

One of the most satisfying shows I played during 1992 was on 31 August at the Chelmsford 'Spectacular' at Hylands Park; it was an outdoor show and there were 24,000 people there. Marty Wilde, the Swinging Blue Jeans and the Merseybeats were also on this bill. It was a beautiful evening, the crowd lined right up the grassy banks – and the sound and feeling of all those people singing 'Ferry' and 'Walk Alone' along with me was really wonderful.

*   *   *

Not everything goes as planned on stage, of course, and I remember a particularly amusing incident when I was in pantomime, in *Jack and the Beanstalk* at Liverpool Empire in 1986. I was Jack, and Kathy Jones, who used to be in 'Coronation Street', was the princess. She was in a cave which the giants had locked her in and you could see prison bars on the window of the stage set. I had to go and rescue her by hitting her with my magic sword, breaking the bars and letting her out. As I hit the window, nothing happened. There was Kathy standing saying, 'Help me, Jack my love, help me' – and nothing happened. So I grabbed hold of the bars and pulled to force the 'window' open. As I did this, the whole pack of scenery fell down on to the stage – and Kathy was left standing on a beer crate. The whole audience were shouting out at this unrehearsed hilarity: 'The princess is pissed!' Only in Liverpool would the kids shout out a great line like that – it could never have been written into the script, but sounded perfect for the moment!

I seem to be particularly accident-prone in my sporting activities. As an example, in 1987 a crowd of us went for a ski-ing visit to Aviemore – Pauline and I took our friends up, and Vicky took hers. But it was a horrendous day for weather, and we decided to go 'curling' instead of ski-ing because the snow condition wasn't fit enough. I kept shouting to the kids, 'Don't go on the ice because if you fall over, you'll hurt yourself. Walk, don't run.' They all got this lecture from me, the big boss. I threw my 'curling board' down on the ice and decided to run after it to see where it was going. I skidded into the air, both feet went up level with my body – and whack I went on to the curling stone and broke four ribs. The kids were shouting, 'Don't run on the ice!'

I spent two weeks in hospital in Inverness. Although the ribs healed nicely, I missed a fortnight's work, which I hate doing.

Shortly afterwards, there was another incident in my sporting antics, as I damaged my finger in my house while dabbling in a bit of Kung Fu and karate. I broke a water sack in the end of my finger. A couple of days later my finger swelled up. It didn't hurt, so I did nothing about it for nearly eighteen months. But in winter when the weather turned cold, my finger would be in agony. So I went to the doctor, who sent me to a specialist, who said it would be a fifteen-minute operation to open up the finger and take away the fluid. Pauline dropped me off for treatment, expecting to collect me after the operation forty minutes later.

However, unknown to me, I had a hiatus hernia, so when they put me under anaesthetic, the fluid came from my stomach into my lungs – and I went away. I was technically, apparently, 'dead' – and this was in the pre-operation room. They dived on me and threw things down my throat to get the fluid out. I knew nothing of this, luckily.

When Pauline returned, the specialist told her they had had a 'slight accident'. He went on to say that I had had 'a bad turn' and suggested she returned a couple of hours later. At that time, she came in and I was in bed with the mask on, all the gear, and I'd been for X-rays. I felt fine apart from having a soar throat from where the pipes had been placed to suck out the fluid. I felt bruised, too.

That night, a nurse came in and said to me, 'Well, can you explain to me what it was like, please?'

I said, 'What d'you mean, love?'

She said, 'Did you have any experiences when you died?'

Well, I nearly died when she told me that. '*What*?' I must have shouted.

She quickly corrected herself. 'No, you didn't, oh, I'm sorry . . .' She didn't realise I had not been informed about it. Technically, I had 'gone' for a short while. As it turned out, it was not to be, so I now know that if there is a Jesus, he didn't want me and neither did the devil. I've been in the land of limbo!

Ski-ing is one of my favourite hobbies and as we were going to Austria one year we decided to go to Llandudno to the dry ski run to practise. About ten friends from the local sports club joined Pauline and me. When we about to begin, Pauline suggested we started halfway up, but I insisted on taking it from the top. On the slope, there were schools of people learning. I got the lift right to the top and decided to come down. This was my first time on a dry ski run and it was much harder to stop, as it turned out, than when there is real snow to press against. Halfway down, I came over one of the 'rises' and saw twelve people lined up in a class. I thought I'd better stop, but quickly realised I couldn't. I went straight through this crowd of a dozen people. Pauline was down at the bottom with our friends and as I reached her she said she'd heard the commotion and told the girls, 'Gerry's on his way down!' She told me I'd knocked this crowd over like ten pins, but luckily nobody was injured. I went back up and apologised to them and they took it in very good spirit.

I was playing for the Showbiz Eleven football team in Guernsey in 1970 and a lot of people had come to see Gerry and the Pacemakers play soccer. As I ran on the pitch, everybody cheered – and I ran up to the ball just before the match began and kicked it hard. But I damaged my hamstring and couldn't play; I was the only one who injured himself before the match. I was carried off with hamstring trouble, stuck on a stretcher – and had to watch the whole of the game while signing autographs.

I have very few phobias, but one is about spiders. Fear is not part of my make-up: I love taking risks and go jet ski-ing and scuba diving. But like a lot of people, I have an inexplicable aversion to spiders of any size.

This reached its zenith in 1983. During some appearances in Gibraltar, I'd been visited by some people from the Gibraltar Tourist Board who asked if I was free two weeks hence. We said that as it happened, we were free, because we never worked in August – but we accepted their invitation for Derek and me to return with our families as their guests, to do some things like help judge the Miss Gibraltar entrant in the Miss World contest, and appear in the beautiful St Michael's Cave. It was a really arduous holiday!

One night, Derek and Debra and Pauline and I were sitting

with our children on the verandah of the Rock Hotel, having dinner under a thatched roof with plants growing under it. I sat facing Derek, Pauline facing Debra. Derek takes up the grisly story:

I saw this spider coming down from the rafter and I don't exaggerate when I say it was as big as my hand. My first reaction was that it was a joke spider. It was on a web and dropping on to Gerry's head – and I truly believed someone was having a joke on him. Except that whoever it was did not know how serious it would be, because Gerry lives in absolute fear of spiders and would definitely kill you if you showed him one in your hand, without knowing he had killed you. It is a genuine phobia.

As it slowly descended towards Gerry's head, I looked straight at him and laughed, and he didn't know why. Then I suddenly realised this was for real and we had a very serious problem.

I knew that if he saw this gigantic spider or if it touched him, this table we were all eating from, all the dinners and drinks and probably the next table, whatever got in his way to get out of this restaurant, would go flying. I knew if he saw this, the scene would be like something nobody in the restaurant had ever seen before. The kids were on the end of our table and to get from our seats was a very tightly knit scene.

I caught Pauline's eye and looked up and drew her eye to the spider while making sure Gerry didn't notice. She went white. By now it was about eight inches from Gerry's head. I suddenly said to Gerry, 'I think it's time the kids went to bed, and it's your turn tonight to take them.'

He said, '*What?*'

Pauline then joined in, urging him to get them upstairs quickly, and there was then a five-minute argument between us, and especially between Pauline and Gerry. But there had to be, to persuade him to get out of there.

Eventually he stormed away from the table, taking the kids

with him. I got someone to take this monster spider away and Gerry returned about ten minutes later, fuming because we had all ganged up on him to send him away to take the kids to bed. We then explained the reason we had to get him out of there. And he literally went into the shakes at the thought of it, the realisation of how near he had been to having this bloody great spider landing on his head.

The number of people around the world who claim to have been 'in my class at school in Liverpool' is unbelievable. One who definitely wasn't, but who gave Derek and me a good laugh, was in Singapore. We were having dinner in a restaurant when a man came up to our table – we thought he was another autograph hunter. But he started a conversation: 'Ah, Jelly. I know you. Jelly and the Pacemakers . . . I love that song you sing, the Pie Song.'

I said, 'Pardon?'

He continued, 'I love the Pie Song you sing.'

I said I was afraid he had me mixed up with someone else and added quite firmly, 'I don't sing a song called the Pie Song.'

Derek and I were already laughing, but he persisted.

'Ah yes you do. I come to your concert tomorrow night and you promise you will sing for me the Pie Song.' Again, I denied it, but he said he had a record of me at home singing this Pie Song.

'OK,' I said, now completely baffled, 'sing it to me.'

'OK,' he said. And he sang in this quavering voice: 'When you walk through a storm, hold your head a-pie.'

'You remember,' he said. 'The Pie Song.'

That night, when I sang it on stage, I realised why he thought it was called 'The Pie Song', as the words 'up high' merge into 'a-pie' if you don't understand English. But when I came off, I said to my interpreter Peter Chinn, who was standing in the wings, 'Peter, you see, it's called "You'll Never Walk Alone".'

His reply was, 'Ah, Gerry, yes – but I prefer "The Pie Song"!'

*   *   *

As a father, I love working with children and one of the most enjoyable periods in my television career was in 1977 when for thirteen weeks, Derek Franks and I appeared on the Thames TV series 'Sooty' in something called 'the Gerry and Derek spot'. We had to write the sketches ourselves, all involving Harry Corbett, and I vividly remember going down with Derek by train to film the first one. He asked me for a look at the scripts I was supposed to have written and of course I was forced to admit I hadn't done them. We wrote the whole series on the train to Euston. They wanted someone to appear in a gorilla skin and I had immediately lumbered Derek into it by saying, 'My manager will do that.' We caused chaos in the studios; at Christmas, we were singing the Slade Christmas song when Derek fell flat on his back on the concrete floor. His eyes were rolling when I picked him up, but we held him upright sufficiently to finish the song in the spirit of 'the show must go on'.

On another occasion, it was my turn to be hurt. In the show, Matthew Corbett and Sooty had a 'laff shop'. My job was to make a point of saying, 'How has Sooty got a laff shop and how do you get a laff out of a shop?' And Matthew replied, 'Well, here's what we do. See all these goodies here? Well, we can get a laff out of them, can't we Sooty?' He nodded, 'Yes.'

I said, 'How do you get a laff out of a custard pie?' With that, Matthew and Sooty picked it up and smashed me in the face with it. All the kids in the theatre went: 'Yeeeeeeaaaaah.' He said, 'Well, that's a laff', and I said, 'How do you get a laff with that big straw hat, then?' Very simply, he said, putting the hat on me, pulling it down hard and smashing it down over my face until the edge of it reached my chin. All the kids roared with laughter, and that was another laff.

'Well,' I continued, 'how do you get a laff with that big sledgehammer?' This hammer had a plastic-coated head and a big wooden handle, and Matthew said, 'I'll show you how!'

As he picked it up and smashed me over the head with it, the wooden handle end, rather than the plastic-coated head, smashed into my head. My face was suddenly covered in the white shaving foam which had been used as the custard pie, mixed with the blood which was now pouring down my face. I looked at him and said, 'Matthew, you've done me!' He collapsed. Poor Sooty nearly died and a voice in the audience shouted, 'Oh, Sooty, you've killed Uncle Gerry!'

I was whipped off to hospital where the doctor immediately asked me what had happened. I said I'd tell him in a minute, because I didn't think he'd believe the details of the story. He took me into the theatre, sat me down, and said I needed five stitches. 'Now tell me what happened,' he insisted.

I said, 'It's a little embarrassing, really. You see, Sooty hit me with a sledgehammer . . .' I reckon that surgeon is still laffing!

The present Pacemakers have been with me for eight years: Andy Cairns on bass guitar, Sean Fitzpatrick on drums and Kevin Jackson on keyboards. They all help with vocals on various songs. Andy was my sound guy when I was going through different line-ups of musicians, but I knew he played bass, so when the time came to restructure the band he was happy to be invited in. Sean and Kevin were introduced to me by a friend who was in one of the old line-ups. These three guys are great. They keep me on my toes and up to date, even though they enjoy playing the old music. I keep my ears open for nice contemporary songs to include in the show – for example, the lovely ballad of recent years by Richard Marx called 'Right Here Waiting' – because it's important to keep my repertoire fresh and current as well as satisfy people's needs for the oldies. The band is as happy as most bands can be on the road, with odd niggles, but nothing that can't be sorted out by sitting down and chatting.

Since 1978, a long-standing follower of Gerry and the Pace-makers, Phil Tucker of Borough Bridge, Yorkshire, has been president of my fan club; having witnessed me at many shows, Phil comments on my attitude to work:

Gerry never forgets that the public has paid his wages. He is a perfectionist. The sound and the lighting have to be just right. Whereas some performers would say, 'All right, let it go at that' at a certain stage, Gerry will get annoyed if it isn't just as he likes it.

I certainly believe in going to great lengths to please the people who put me where I am. I've no time for the cynical attitude that some artists have, or the 'big time' feeling that signing autographs or handing out photographs to people is somehow tiresome. To me, that's exactly why we all came into show business in the first place, to secure a loyal audience, and I always find time for people who have been good enough to take an interest in me.

At a certain stage in a show-business career, the record scene quietens down for most artists. Even the biggest names stop making huge hits like they used to. So you have to accept this and as long as you can stay in the business, that's fine.

Records don't matter if you work on a good stage act; people will come and see the show. The records they remember you by, they still enjoy. I believe crowds become a bit frightened of an artist making a record they don't like, and that's why they stop buying them at a certain point. They are familiar with certain songs that will forever be associated with you, and they don't want those memories to be interfered with. In fact, they would rather you didn't bother recording again: 'Leave it as it was; don't make a new record' – I'm sure that's their unspoken feeling.

If all the thousands of people I meet a year on tour want me to make a record, why don't they ask me when my next one is coming out? They don't – so we make records now because we like to do so, because we enjoy trying new ideas, but if it doesn't get in the charts it doesn't break my heart. It's not the be-all and end-all; I sometimes find recording boring.

So I go on stage to entertain. People pay to come and see a show. They enjoy the memories. Kids of eleven come up to me after the show and say, 'Great show, lovely music.'

I still get a genuine thrill from performing. Half an hour or so before the show starts, Colin Waterworth, my driver and assistant, pours me a Cinzano and soda in the dressing room. I have a joke with the lads; I relax and like to talk about something light – cricket, tennis, golf, sex. Nothing to do with work. But I cannot wait to get on.

During the ten seconds while I'm waiting for the 'gate' to open, I'm like a greyhound in a trap waiting to be set free. Then it's time for me to run on stage and swank again. It's straightforward showing off – the same factor that motivated me when I was a kid at school – and I enjoy it. I think every artist has got to enjoy showing off. That's the very nature of getting on a stage and wanting people to listen to you perform. It's no place to be if you're shy.

After all these years, if I didn't have that enthusiasm, I would be in trouble. Because sometimes, the venue doesn't feel too good, or the dressing-room facilities are abominable, or the organisation isn't good. I pull myself out of any worries like that by telling myself and the band that we can't let the public suffer. They've come to see the show. They don't know or care that the dressing room's crap!

Some artists seem to go on stage reluctantly, saying they prefer the recording studio. I hate that attitude. So they shouldn't get on stage, where they have agreed to perform for people. The true entertainers – the late, great Sammy Davis Junior, Bruce Forsyth, Bob Monkhouse, people of that calibre – know the rules of the business. They are there for the public.

There was a song called 'The Big Black Giant', which seemed to portray the audience as exactly that, in the eyes of an entertainer, something to fear. To me, it's not a Black Giant at all, but a room full of friends. I've never worried about an audience. They are supporters who have paid to come and see me help them have a good time. I get on stage, and to me, it's a party. 'Hello, how are you, welcome, enjoy yourself.' And I always come off knackered, bathed in sweat, but if they've applauded, it was a great night.

Pauline has seen how much I need to work to be happy. 'The stage is like a drug to him,' she believes. My travelling these days is extensive – at least 50,000 miles a year around Britain alone – but I love the end of each journey – stage or home. As Pauline says:

Maybe we've gone out for a night or had a late night and he's got up next morning, tired, and he says, 'God, I've got to go to . . . today' and I can see he doesn't want to go, dreads it. He gets himself ready and organised and gets off in the car and he rings all the time from the car; he has a thing about the phone; he has to have this contact with me; he phones a dozen times on a journey. The minute he gets there and sees the stage, he's wide awake. Forgets he's tired, he didn't feel like doing it; it's gone, and he's alive on that stage.

Pauline has had to rap my knuckles a few times for being still 'on stage' when I get back home from a show:

He used to come home sometimes and say, 'Get me this' or 'While you're there, do that,' and I'd reply, 'Hey, you're not talking to one of the group now.' And he'd realise. He used to try it on, but I never let him do it now. And he knows. He's held on to his roots and he's proud of them.

When I get home after the 'high' of performing, I can be a bit tetchy. As Pauline says:

His mum and dad are still in Toxteth and they won't stand any messing from him. If he swears in front of them, she still tells him off. They've never put him on a pedestal. He's just their son . . . and that's the way he likes it. This is what's helped to keep his feet on the ground. I've done that, too. I have fought to do that.

After ninety-nine per cent of my shows, Colin drives me home to the Wirral, whatever time we finish. I've seen enough hotel rooms to last me for ever and I prefer to feel I'm back where I belong. To quote Pauline again:

The home is Gerry's anchor. He doesn't enjoy the travelling itself much, but he never deliberately stays away if he can get back after a show. Sometimes, I've been with him to, say, Bristol, and I've sat in the back of the car thinking, 'This is a long way . . . but we've got to do the *same journey* to get home *after* the show.' But Gerry does that *every night*!

In my life away from show business, I'm stubborn and a strict disciplinarian with my daughters, according to Pauline. (Victoria Ann, our second daughter, was born on 27 January 1980.) That's true, and it might be because I'm strict with myself.

'A lot of our friends are quite shocked,' Pauline says, 'because they think coming from show business he might be more open-minded, easy-going. But he's not. He's very old-fashioned morally and very strict with the girls. He's softer with Vicky than he was with Yvette, but he'll still only take so much. People have the opinion that because he's seen it all and he lives in the world of rock 'n' roll and has travelled the world, he will be relaxed about life – and they're surprised about how strict he can be.'

The funny thing about Vicky was that Pauline had been told after the birth of our first child that she would not conceive again. So we told ourselves that at least we had one lovely daughter and continued on our merry way. Then, fourteen years later, came a surprise. Pauline told me she was pregnant.

'Don't be daft, you can't be,' I said. But the doctor confirmed it and we said, 'Blooming heck, that's great!'

Vicky was born by Caesarean section and was such a lovely surprise to us that we considered her a gift from God. Maybe because of the circumstances of her arrival, I *am* a little more patient with her than I was with Yvette.

Both Pauline and I were raised in very strong Catholic families and we are firm believers in God. We think that it was perhaps because we both had such an extremely religious childhood that we stopped going to church later as a kind of reaction to that intensity, but we still believe and we want our children to do the same. Pauline felt brainwashed; she went to a convent school and had two hours' religious homework every night.

The one person I will take criticism from, particularly about my show, has always been Pauline.

'He's very stubborn and argues the points I make,' she says, 'and he will never say I was right, but next time I go to his show, I will notice he has often made the change I suggested. I've always thrown my pennyworth in; and he never tells me to shut up and mind my own business.' I think that's fair; at home, Pauline is in charge.

One of the worst sides of my life on the road has been my diet. Show business brings erratic timekeeping, and one of the rules is that we should eat properly. Pauline has been battling with me for years over my eating habits.

If Pauline gave me a meal at 5 p.m. and I was going on stage at 10 p.m., I couldn't perform; and that's the basis of my problem.

When I'm due on stage at night, I hardly eat anything all day; I have no breakfast, might stop on the road for a sandwich, then get to the hotel and might have a bowl of soup (no bread). Then on the way home after the show I'll stop for fish and chips – and be creased with indigestion all night, every night! For many years I went all day and into a late show on a pint of milk and an apple. In recent years, after the show, I have usually eaten nothing until I get home in the early hours, when I have meat-paste sandwiches and a pint of milk. Pauline has been fighting me on this since I started this routine shortly after our marriage; I never have a proper knife-and-fork meal when I've got a show to do. Pauline often wonders how I've survived and says she thinks I must sometimes feel sick with hunger, but those meat-paste sandwiches and milk at night (the worst thing that you can do, eat like that before going to bed) have been a very hard habit to break. I'm still working on it.

I hate the drugs scene. I despise the fact that drugs infiltrated rock 'n' roll. I always felt strongly against it because I went round hospitals and saw kids of sixteen, brain-dead from drugs. It was frightening.

In the 1960s, when a lot of rock stars started using drugs, so many people thought, 'Hey, man, this is what's happening. Cool, baby, rock on.' I saw friends in the music business dying or losing their brains or destroying their talent, and I started preaching against it as often as I could to get people off it. I still do and I always will. If I see kids whom I think may be going that way, I lecture them. I see it as a duty, as one who's seen so much damage caused by drugs.

It's difficult to convert people who are using drugs, so I try to warn people against starting. By the time the Beatles began with it in the mid-1960s, I knew it was useless having conversations with them about it. I said to myself, 'Idiots!' – and I was proved right, because their weakest songs were written while they were indulging. Luckily for them, they didn't get deeply into it to the point of self-destruction . . . but look at the number of those who did, stars and non-stars. You can look around today and see survivors who are in a horrendous condition. They came through it, but still didn't win the fight. They're only half human.

I look at my family and thank God none of us have ever been involved. I urge everyone to give drugs a wide berth. I always say to people who are on the edge of it: look to life, look to yourself. Do something more important. Life's hard enough without walking around in a mist asking where you are, who you are, what you did yesterday – and not knowing the answers.

6

Tragedies and Triumphs

Magic Moments

John Lennon was a genius; Paul McCartney still is. They were totally different people and I could tell in one second flat who had written which song. John didn't ever give a crap about audiences, whereas Paul always loved them and still needs to get on stage. I loved John and Paul for entirely different reasons: John for his nitty-gritty, razor-like voice, even on ballads he wrote like 'In My Life', and Paul's soft touch and that ability to write a straight love song – and surprise us. I envy him that.

It would be a very dangerous mistake to underestimate Paul. I was in Australia doing a radio interview in 1977 when the announcer told me he was going to play the new McCartney single.

'What's it called?' I asked eagerly.

'"Mull of Kintyre",' he told me.

I thought it sounded a strange title for a Macca single and when it finished playing I was asked, on air, what I thought of it. I said, 'Well, I've never heard such a load of crap in my life. It won't be a hit. You're a mug, Paul, making that!'

But how wrong can anyone be! It became one of the biggest selling records of all time, proving again how brilliantly commercial Paul's touch has always been.

He is terrifying and I don't know where he gets it from. And I admire the way he's always trying to do new things, like for example the 'Liverpool Oratorio'. I'd never be surprised to find him turning out another masterpiece like 'Yesterday' tomorrow; come to think of it, that's not a bad title for a song. 'Yesterday Tomorrow' – for Sixties people everywhere.

When we were all much younger, I could always visualise Paul as an artist and a man who would mature as he did, married and with a family. I could also see Cilla in my mind's eye as married, appearing on television as an all-round entertainer just as Brian Epstein predicted, settled down with a family. I could never see Cilla 'on the road', as she was never a concert-touring person like me.

But John Lennon was always different in my mind and remains so in my memory. I just knew I'd never see him grow old. I had this terrible feeling about it, right back when we were both in our twenties and moving around Liverpool together. He was wacky and so was I and the sick sense of humour we shared was part of our growing up, but even as a young guy there was something slightly worrying about him. It was like he was racing through life. He didn't have the look of a man who would be happy in maturity.

As an artist, he was absolutely unique. I recorded some of his special songs, 'Imagine', 'Woman' and the song most people identify with the period just before he was killed, '(Just Like) Starting Over'.

He went through a bad stage but I thought his final album, *Double Fantasy*, showed he was on the way back to producing some great stuff. He obviously wanted to rebuild himself. While I wasn't expecting him to live to a ripe old age, I was shattered by the horrendous way in which he died.

The news reached me at five o'clock in the morning on 9 December 1980; the phone rang at my home. It was Radio City, the Liverpool station with whom I've always been closely involved.

'We've just had a message from the States,' they said. 'John is dead.'

Like everybody else in the world, I found the news just

unbelievable. I said they should check such a terrible statement very carefully before announcing it on the radio. Then I went back to sleep. It wasn't the kind of news I expected to turn out to be true.

A couple of hours later, I awoke, turned to Pauline and said, 'Did you hear me on the phone earlier?'

'Yes,' she replied. 'They've shot John Lennon.'

'So I wasn't dreaming?'

'No, John's dead.'

I was in a state of great shock. My mind started racing, thinking of the times I had phoned John and of the stupid things we had said to each other, even when he'd settled in New York. When I was appearing in that city, I'd called him once after a gap of a few years of not communicating and he came on the phone with the words, 'How are ya, daft arse?' That was the way we spoke to each other, just as if the days at the Seamen's Mission in Hamburg hadn't gone.

I reflected on how John and I, as young men in Hamburg and in Liverpool, would walk around sending up and winding up everybody in sight, especially minorities. We enjoyed taking the mickey out of people, enjoying being rude to people together, as rebellious kids do (and particularly in Liverpool).

The only thing to do that horrible day was carry on with some kind of routine to get rid of the shock. I had to go to Bradford for a meeting. Loads of radio and television people were calling me; I went in to appear on the Yorkshire TV programme 'Calendar' to chat about my memories and thoughts of John. And I sang 'Imagine'.

I had a real feeling of loss. Even if I didn't ring John every week or month, he had been there to ring. But no more. I was really sad to think that no longer would I hear that miserable, nasal, rasping, shouting, moaning voice down the phone. He was always grumbling, but that was John. I was annoyed to lose a man of that great talent who would definitely have left us a lot more of himself through his music. After his bad years, he was sounding fresh in his writing again and I always loved to hear the real John Lennon gear. God knows what he'd be doing now; it could have been amazing because he certainly had the ability. I'm sad still to know that I'll never hear that voice again till I join him in that Cavern in the sky.

Show business has been very good to me and I firmly believe in giving back something to the public, especially by way of charity work when the cause is a good one. The public gave me what I and my family have today and one of the ways I can repay is by doing what I do for worthwhile British charities; it's dead easy to do, costs us nothing, and helps people who desperately need our free performances.

But I could never have predicted the scale in which I'd be involved in two fund-raising projects in the 1980s, both related to football and both arising from such huge disasters that you get the chills just thinking about them.

The first was on 11 May 1985, when the whole of Britain, especially soccer fans and their families, were stunned by the tragedy at the Valley Parade ground, home of Bradford football club. Fifty-six people died and many more were injured when the stand caught fire; it touched everybody and particularly those of us who'd been soccer fans all our lives. Derek Franks, who lived not far from the ground at that time, could actually go out into his garden and see the flames, and the television commentator was in tears as he described the severity of the blaze with the inevitable consequences of human tragedy.

I said to Derek that we should make a record to help the families of the victims, because horrific stories were coming in of people who would be in real trouble; by buying our record, people who felt helpless would feel they were doing something specific. Debra, Derek's wife, had already suggested a 'charity single' to him – and he was quick off the mark in calling round to a load of celebrities in London to see if they'd chip in by giving their services free.

The original idea had been for me to sing 'You'll Never Walk Alone' with the Bradford football team; Derek discussed this with Trevor Cherry, their manager, but they were not keen. They probably had other things on their mind, but we were well down the line in arranging for show-business people to help and we'd secured the co-operation of Ray Levy, who was the executive producer of the project, and Spartan Records, who gave all their services and facilities free.

As we drove to London for the recording session, I said to Derek, 'I don't suppose many people will turn up; I'm going to be just about on my own in this studio.' But the turnout of artists was simply stupendous, right across the range of show business, from light entertainment to heavy rock artists. Everybody really got into the spirit of the good cause: their names are on the record under the name The Crowd, which is what we called ourselves.

The variety of music represented was wonderful: we had Tony Christie and Rick Wakeman, the Liverpool boxer John Conteh who's a dear friend of mine, and the Barron Knights, Jess Conrad and Kiki Dee, Bruce Forsyth and the Foxes (the three daughters of the Beverly Sisters), Rolf Harris and Graham Gouldman, Kenny Lynch and Keith Chegwin, Tony Hicks, Colin Blunstone, Tim Hinkley, Rolf Harris, Johnny Logan, Ringo Starr's son Zak Starkey, Girls School, Black Lace, John Otway, Gary Holton, Peter Cook, the Nolans, John Entwistle, Motorhead, Karen Clark, disc jockeys Dave Lee Travis, Graham Dene and Ed Stewart, Phil Lynott, Smokie, Joe Fagan, Eddie Harding, Gerard Kenny, Chris Robinson, Tim Healey, Kin Kelly, John Verity, Rose Marie, David Shilling, Chris Norman, Pete Spencer, Bernie Winters and a load of others who gave their time, energy and money to this project.

The 'B' side of the record featured messages, and for this I was glad that Paul McCartney contributed some nicely spoken words to add to the record's strength. There was a great atmosphere in the studio and I was really pleased so many of my friends had turned out for this cause. We had some fun making it and by the time we reached the mixing stage, word came that we were guaranteed the number one position in the charts on advance orders alone. It was in the shops within ten days; during that time, I visited the Valley Parade ground to see the charred debris and the shrines of wreaths, crosses and flowers commemorating the deaths of the victims. I also visited St Luke's Hospital, where the victims were, and it was choking to see and hear little girls of eleven and twelve years old who had been badly scarred in the fire. When I spoke to some of them, typical remarks were, 'Gerry, will I ever be pretty?'

I said, 'You bet your life you will. Our money will help to make sure you are pretty when you come out of here.'

Fifty-six people were dead from the fire; we couldn't help them, but we could focus on those who survived, and the relatives of the victims.

The record went to the number four position at first, then jumped to the number one on 1 June 1985. We quickly sold more than 300,000 singles and the early estimate that we'd be able to give £50,000 was overtaken by an estimate of nearly three times that amount. For me, the whole operation was doubly pleasing: the song that I'd casually put into my act back in Hamburg to provide a contrast with rock 'n' roll, and which gave me a number one in 1963, was now really working as a football anthem in a positive way to help people. It was also the first time any artist had re-recorded a number one hit and taken it back to the top of the chart.

Eventually the single made about £132,000. We'd always said we didn't want to give the money out in bits and pieces, but to wait until it had all come in, gathered in to a substantial amount, and then contribute a large cheque to the Disaster Appeal. Six months after our record project, Derek Franks phoned to say the cash was ready and to suggest a meeting with the fund organisers. Their reply was surprising to say the least: 'We don't want it.'

'Pardon,' said Derek.

'We've closed the Disaster Appeal and we don't want it,' they said.

Pointing out that the money could not be ignored because the

British public had sent the record to number one on the basis that their cash would help the victims and their families, Derek and I had to find a method of using the funds constructively. We were lucky. We met a surgeon, David Sharp, who had attended a lot of the injured, and two worthwhile destinations were found for the profits. A burns research unit was opened in Bradford, and supporting that was totally in keeping with the nature of the tragedy; and the money also went into research towards what became known as 'the Rocker's Arm' or the 'Bradford Sling', a unique method of support to aid recovery for broken arms and wrists, which was a big problem resulting from the injuries sustained in the fire. By coincidence, six years after the disaster, Derek's wife Debra found the 'Bradford Sling' a great benefit when she sustained some nasty injuries after falling from a horse, so we have first-hand knowledge and experience of the fillip the money has provided in the medical world.

There were a couple of sad aspects to the project: we were disappointed to be told that the music publishers of 'You'll Never Walk Alone' would not waive their rights to royalties from every record we sold; they would have made a lot of money from the project and we felt strongly that on occasions like this, a bit more heart would have sent a load more money to the people who needed it. And when, in 1991, David Sharp told us that the money had been exhausted, Derek got in touch with the Alhambra Theatre, Bradford (which is corporation-run) and asked for free use of the place to stage a celebrity concert to re-boost the funds of the charity – they said the Alhambra could be hired at a cost of £6,000.

The finale to all this is that obviously the money never went to the people it was directly intended for, victims of the Bradford fire, but it certainly wasn't wasted and went to a wider cause. Our efforts were not in vain, and I'd do the same thing the same way tomorrow.

Exactly four years later, a second British sports disaster struck – unbelievably, it was again innocent crowds at a soccer match who were either killed or badly injured. This one was closer to home for me, for the dreadful crush at Hillsborough football ground, where Nottingham Forest were playing Liverpool, was a bitter experience for anyone living on Merseyside; it was clear from the earliest reports that hundreds would be dead or injured and we were witnessing a truly terrible tragedy. Having been a Liverpool football fan since I was a lad, I was shattered; like so many Merseysiders, I just sat down and cried when I heard the news.

The story was on every television programme and on the front pages and nearly every inside page of the national newspapers, but around Liverpool, it was like wartime all over again; the sheer horror of people who knew someone who'd just gone to a football match and then got crushed to death couldn't fail to chill us. The death toll was ninety-five.

Once again, the best thing show-business people like me could do was offer a little entertainment by way of a free gift, to raise some essential funds. I knew immediately that I should be involved in a new project; there was some early talk of re-releasing The Crowd's 'You'll Never Walk Alone', but we quickly rejected that. Derek and I felt that the record was made especially for the Bradford disaster and to re-release it would be damaging in two ways: it would be a slap in the face to the Bradford victims, and it would re-open old wounds.

This was a colossal Liverpool human disaster, too, so I felt the record should be Scouse-flavoured in every way. At that time, I'd been doing some sessions with Pete Waterman of the record producers Stock, Aitken and Waterman and I phoned him with my ideas. We'd met about a year earlier at a party thrown by Terry Smith, the boss of Liverpool's Radio City, where Pete was also disc jockeying a Saturday morning radio programme.

I told Pete of my wish to do a benefit record; he immediately jumped at the idea and said he'd produce and release it free. That was a good start.

He asked me what song I wanted to do and I said, '"Ferry", because it's Liverpool ... I wrote it about Liverpool people and I feel that is the song we should be doing for this disaster.'

He said, 'No, I'd rather write you a new one', and I said, 'OK, do that, let me listen to it and we'll see. If you want to write one about Liverpool, that's fine.'

Pete rang me the following day and said, 'I'm sorry, you're right. I've listened again to "Ferry". We couldn't write anything more Liverpool than that.'

The idea for a Hillsborough fund-raising record struck an immediate chord in the hearts of the three Liverpool artists we quickly approached to join me: Paul McCartney, Holly Johnson of Frankie Goes To Hollywood, and the hot Liverpool band the Christians. It was a team effort from Stock, Aitken and Waterman – Pete led the project, though, and his recollections of the record, and the early difficulties he had with me as the songwriter, are interesting:

> They didn't go into the studio together here at PWL in the Borough, London, because it would have caused too much chaos. Gerry came in and sang it all through at first, just in case anybody couldn't remember the tune; the Christians and Paul McCartney went in together; Holly Johnson was in Germany and couldn't get back until the day after everybody else had finished their vocals. Once we'd got all the vocals, we duplicated the others where we liked them and swapped them in and out where we thought each sang the best.
>
> It was a difficult production as far as Gerry was concerned because he had been singing this song he wrote for twenty years and he had a pre-conception of what it should sound like before we started. We had a little bit of trouble with Gerry on it; he and I have a mutual friend, the boss of Radio City, Terry Smith, and Gerry phoned him to voice doubts that we would be able to treat his song differently and successfully. He thought I had not grasped the way he saw the song.
>
> The way we do things is that the artists sing to a track that's not the final track. The minute we've got all the voices on, we

take all the backing off and re-lay everything. That's the way we work; so when a singer sings the song he never hears the record. So when Gerry sang 'Ferry', he was just really singing to rough chords and rough rhythms – so he went away with this misconception that it would be this bloody awful record he had sung to. I had tried to reassure him with 'Look, Gerry, don't worry about it. This is the start. When we've got all the vocals on, and we know where everybody's going to sing, then we'll start again and put it all together and take it from there. We'll find the *emotion* that comes out in people's voices and we'll let that come through by heightening or lowering the track at that point, or taking everything else out.'

It was a bit difficult to try to explain that to Gerry. It was a shock to him because he'd sung it every night for twenty years and it was his possession and suddenly we had our hands on it and what we wanted was different from what he wanted. He wrote it as a *pop song*. When we produced it with four artists, we did it as a *tribute*, which changed the whole meaning of why the song was being recorded. Gerry had recorded it with George Martin as a hit; we were now recording it with Paul McCartney and everybody else to raise money for a charity. We were creating an emotional message to wrench money out of people's pockets. Our job was to make money for an appeal and for that we had to be mercenary.

Paul, Holly and the Christians never had any worries about their sessions because they each had a totally different perspective of the song; they were coming new to it.

The whole operation had been pulled together by Pete with tremendous speed. After he'd checked to see if the bereaved families actually wanted it to be done, the recording session had been put in place within forty-eight hours of the disaster. Within two weeks the record was finished and every radio station in Britain agreed that the first play (apart from on news bulletins) should be by Liverpool's Radio City on Pete Waterman's Saturday show. That was the first time I heard it, too, such was the speed of its completion. I didn't like it at first, because it was hard to recognise my old song with such a new treatment, but I quickly realised it was a powerful sound with precisely what I'd wanted all along: a Scouse flavour.

One of the interesting stories about the record concerns the middle in which Paul McCartney lets out a wail. As Pete Waterman recalls:

> He goes out of tune and he wanted me to take it off and do it again and I wouldn't let him. I said, 'Why did you do it?' and he said, 'Well, it's just how I felt.' And I said, 'Then it stays!' Linda McCartney called me up afterwards and said, 'You know, you're probably the only person who's ever told Paul McCartney that he couldn't have his own way. But all of us down here think you're absolutely right; we think it's marvellous to hear him showing some emotion.' And Paul to this day tells people that Pete Waterman is the only guy who's told him to shut his gob.

Pete says he insisted on leaving it in because he knew that he'd captured a piece of magic on the tape:

> He wanted to make it perfect which, of course, because he's Paul McCartney, he would do. But we knew the song had got to him at that point, the emotion of the tragedy had got to him, and when you see the video it definitely gets your throat, catches you and gives you a tear in the eye. McCartney did capture the spirit of it – and that's down to the fact that Gerry wrote a great song that does stand up to that treatment.

The record went straight to number one on 20 May 1989 and sold 800,000 singles. It sold many hundreds of thousands more on albums and compilation albums and the money is still coming in. The Hillsborough Fund raised £13 million and a staggering half of that, approximately, came from 'Ferry Cross the Mersey'. Every penny went to the charity and the victims' families through a fund called Mersey Aid.

It has been heart-warming to reflect that a simple, pretty song about Liverpool which I had written as I was driving Pauline to dinner twenty years earlier has become such an important vehicle with which to help so many people. And it was fun to think that Paul McCartney had returned, with me, to the top of the chart with a Marsden composition; but then, a few years earlier, I'd shown my regard for Paul and John Lennon's songs with an album called *The Lennon-McCartney Songbook*.

That year, 1989, was tragic for football, but also moving in the spirit it generated. I was in Hong Kong on a concert tour when I received an invitation from the Football Association to sing 'You'll Never Walk Alone' before the all-Merseyside Cup Final between Liverpool and Everton at Wembley. After some persuasion of the Hong Kong concert organisers, Derek Franks arranged for me to cut short my dates there and fly home a day early. I flew into Heathrow and had three hours' sleep in a hotel before going to Wembley. Back in Hong Kong they had hardly believed the reason for the abrupt ending of the tour, but when they tuned in to world television and saw me on the Wembley pitch, they contacted Derek to say they now believed our reason for returning to London.

With the disaster still very strong in everybody's minds, this was both an honour and the most nerve-wracking experience of my life. My knees must have shaken for about six hours before I reached the podium, which says a lot, because I don't normally suffer from nerves before getting on any stage. But this was something very different and important in human terms.

Liverpool and Everton supporters were at different ends of the stadium. To thank the Everton supporters for being so kind after the Hillsborough tragedy, I first turned and bowed to them and they gave me the most tremendous cheer I'd had in my life. I then turned to my right and bowed to the Liverpool supporters, who gave me the same cheer.

The beautiful aspect of that day, which I shall never forget, was that both teams' supporters sang 'Walk Alone'. As I began singing, the crowd was wonderful in showing the warmth of the occasion, and with such a response I simply floated. The moment was televised worldwide and solidified the song as soccer's unofficial anthem.

In my speech, I said I was at Wembley for three reasons. First, to mark the memory of those who could not be at that Cup Final, because they had died in a recent tragedy. Secondly, to thank everyone for coming, Evertonians as well as Liverpudlians, for the massive support they had given throughout to Liverpool fans in the terrible aftermath of the tragedy. And thirdly, to prove to the world that Everton and Liverpool supporters get on well with each other.

That day stands as one of the most emotional in my life.

In show business we are very lucky to be able to help people, and the best way to do this is via the many charities that cannot get help from the government. I'm very conscious of the fact that while people like me try to do our best with public appearances, concerts and making records, there's a huge number of people who work day in, day out, to organise these charities.

To mention a few I am associated with, there is Riding for the Disabled; the Paraplegic Weightlifting Team based in Stoke Manderville, of which I am the vice president; the Variety Club of Great Britain; all the brain scanner appeals around the country; the Royal Society for the Prevention of Cruelty to Children; the workshops for the blind; and the Merseyside Accommodation Project which we are working on to give kids who are homeless a chance to live in someone's house and get back on their feet. There's also the Home Farm Trust to help spastics and, in Liverpool, Age Concern; and Claire House, a respite home which will be built in Liverpool for sick children. And I'd like to thank again everybody who helped us to support the Bradford fire disaster and Hillsborough football ground tragedy. I'll always do what's possible for charities, but it's important to thank all the people who make them tick.

On a lighter side, I'm president of the Scousers Down Under Club in Australia, where there seems to be a surprising number of expatriate Liverpudlians. In 1992, the crummy old stand at the Kemlyn Road part of Anfield football ground was knocked down to make way for a new one, and Arthur Johnson of the Liverpool *Echo* had the bright idea of getting the famous Liver Bird sign from the old stand and having me take it down to Australia. There, I presented it as a souvenir to the many Scousers I met during my autumn 1992 Australian tour.

For any entertainer, being the subject of television's 'This Is Your Life' is a big accolade and I never had the faintest expectation that I would be chosen for that programme. But in 1985 the producers began their elaborate plan to feature my life story and of course the whole idea of the show is that the celebrity should know nothing of the project until he's whisked into the studio before the cameras. This element of surprise is vital to the show's impact, and my wife Pauline and Derek Franks were the chief organisers of the plot to get me to London for the programme, while kidding me that I was going for something else. October 26 1985 was one of the craziest nights of my life.

As Derek recalls:

> When I got a call from Thames TV saying they wanted Gerry for the show, I said there was no way on earth I'd get him down there without a strong reason. I suggested that reason might be a 'pretend' appearance on 'Give Us A Clue', because he'd been saying for months before that he wanted to do that programme. This was the excuse we planned as a decoy to get Gerry to London, and he readily agreed to the date I gave him.

As the date drew near, Pauline had a difficult situation with our daughter, Vicky, who was then five and had brought school photographs home which I always paid for. These school photographs always arrived at half-term time, and Pauline knew that if I was asked for money for them, I would know that the time had come to go to Anglesey for a week with her and Vicky. Pauline says:

I had to hide these photographs, but the whole thing went wrong when Vicky said to him, 'Look, Daddy, I've got my school photos.'

Gerry said, 'Well, here you are, there's the money, you can hand it in on Monday when you go to school.'

And Vicky said, 'I'm not in school on Monday, it's my half term.'

Immediately, Gerry picked up the phone to Derek and said, 'You can forget "Give Us A Clue". Vicky's off school. We're going to Anglesey.'

Derek and Pauline then began sneaky conversations to discuss how they were going to get me to change my mind. 'The more you pressure Gerry, the more determined he is to stick by his guns,' Pauline points out. 'But his Achilles heel is Vicky. So we used her. We told him how all her friends at school loved "Give Us A Clue" and how proud his daughter would be when Vicky's friends told her they'd seen her dad on the show. We knew he'd give in to something that would please Vicky like this.'

The night before the programme, Derek and I drove down to a London hotel where we met up with the producer, Daphne Shadwell, who had worked with us on the 'Sooty' series. She was in on the deception and we all pretended to rehearse for 'Give Us A Clue' next day. There was another small difficulty: as Derek says, before any television programme, I don't drink but prefer an early night:

I wanted Gerry drunk so that next morning he'd stay in bed late while there was a rehearsal for 'This Is Your Life'. At nine o'clock, he said, 'We're going to bed now', but I said, 'No, we'll have another bottle of wine.' I made him continue drinking and he thought I'd gone off my trolley because he knew he had a major television show next day and he could not understand why I was making him drink.

As we drove to the Teddington Lock studios, I was telling Derek which way to go without realising that he was following a car which was in radio contact with 'This Is Your Life' and Eamonn Andrews. Derek was ignoring my directions, something I wasn't used to! I began to bark at him as he drove. As we arrived at the gateway to Thames TV, the barrier was down and Derek announced to the commissionaire: 'Gerry Marsden for "Give Us A Clue".' I didn't hear the man's reply, luckily, because he said to Derek out of my earshot, 'It's not "Give Us A Clue" tonight, it's "This Is Your Life".'
Derek says:

Next, Gerry told me where to park the car. I ignored him and, as instructed by the 'This Is Your Life' people earlier, parked in the middle of the car park. Gerry was now having a seizure in the car, telling me I'd parked wrongly. As he opened the door, the lights went on, the music started, and he nearly had a heart attack on that spot.

I really was in a state of shock. They'd lied completely to me, and it had worked brilliantly. As they began playing my music loudly with the lights beating down on me, I thought a bomb had gone off, with that impact. I leaned over the car to Derek and cursed him for his trickery. But of course, as the programme unfolded and so many of my relatives and friends and musicians came forward under the compèring of Eamonn Andrews, it became a tremendously emotional night for me. I really didn't have a clue until it happened, but I was glad they'd duped me into it!

People often ask me what is the most embarrassing moment I have had on stage. It's difficult because there are so many unusual events in my memory but one, particularly embarrassing and a bit of a disaster for me, occurred in 1990.

We were in Halifax at the end of a thirty-five-date tour with Lulu. I jumped up on stage and spun my body round, as I usually do when I return for an encore. As I did so, I felt a terrible pain in the back of my leg. What I'd actually done, it transpired later, was rip the Achilles tendon in my calf. Luckily, it was the last song in the show, the rock 'n' roller 'Rip It Up'. I finished, took my bows, staggered off stage into the wings and screamed, 'Aaaaaaaargh' with pain. 'I've done my leg,' I shouted. They carried me to the dressing room and put some cold water on it and I travelled home.

When I arrived in the very early hours of the morning, nobody was up. Pauline was in bed but not asleep, but I had no idea she was awake. I couldn't walk up the stairs because by now the pain was excruciating, so I had to climb up backwards on my bum. My right leg was in the worst agony I've ever experienced. I eventually pulled myself along the landing rail into our bedroom – and there was Pauline sitting up in bed with a face like poison!

'Where have you been until this time?' she said, 'and look at the state of you!'

I explained that I'd been nowhere except to Halifax for work and I'd been trying to get upstairs for ages. She had thought I was stoned out of my brain and couldn't get up the stairs for that reason! When she realised I wasn't bluffing she stuck me in a cold bath to relieve the pain.

Next day we were in Glasgow, so I rang Brian Scott, a friend who's the physiotherapist for the Celtic football team. He had a look at it before I went to the show and made me a special bandage that enabled me to walk, but not far. So I had to go on stage that night with a pair of crutches.

At the sight of me, the Glasgow audiences, who are quite wonderful, shouted things like: 'Ah, Jim lad, where's your parrot?' When I explained that I'd done my leg, they had a bit of sympathy for me; the show went ahead, but I played the guitar sitting on a bar stool. When the time came for me to go over to the piano for the section of the show when I play that, I thought it would be great, because I could then relax my body. I was never more wrong.

As we started thumping out rock 'n' roll songs, the stand cap collapsed on the piano, the piano fell down on my legs, and I was stuck under the piano on the stage, screaming, still trying to sing. The audience loved it. As I was dragged off stage, they said I should keep the accident in the show, it was so great. We finished the show professionally, but those were two extraordinary concerts. It took six months of physiotherapy to get my leg back to normal.

I've very few regrets thus far in life, but one small one is not being able to read music. The way we rock 'n' rollers began was by steaming in and trusting our heads to get the sound right. It must be better to be able to read music, as my daughters Yvette and Vicky do, and I'd definitely like to be able to sit down in any band and be faced with a piece of music I could immediately read and play.

I'm a good listener, though, and a great believer also in 'every man to his own job'. If a producer has ever told me during the making of a record to rephrase something, I reckon he's paid to know that what he's suggested is for the benefit of the record. I'll argue if I feel he's really wrong, but never for the sake of it.

And so, in my career as in my life, it's full circle. It began almost as a fairy tale in the 1960s, then I had a difficult time in the 1970s, and that required me to fight back. My 1980s were good and the 1990s are better because Derek Franks reckons I will never admit defeat on any subject whatsoever, and that's true; my aggressive Liverpool background always brings out the fighter instinct in me. Derek says my attitude is that attack is the best method of defence, and in summing up that aspect of me he adds:

If Gerry worked in a normal job and heard he was going to be sacked, he would resign before they sacked him, or he'd go further down the road and give them an even better reason to sack him. That fighting spirit has carried him through his career. If he does or says something and it's wrong and it's proved to be wrong, Gerry will twist things round very cleverly to show that he was never defeated, ever.

I think that's an important method of surviving in life as much as in show business: I expect a lot from myself, particularly persistence and determination, and I want them also from those around me. I've been lucky, both in my family and my colleagues.

I'd like to continue performing as long as Frank Sinatra has done. What would I retire *to*? I already play golf, go on holiday to our homes in Anglesey and Spain, and make myself a nuisance around the house when I'm back on the Wirral. I'd get no extra fun from retirement; too much sitting on my bum and gardening wouldn't suit me, although I quite like to potter. I prefer to be busy and keep to a schedule.

I've got a plan to make a comedy film and I have an idea for a stage musical, but I can take my time with these things. In all my thirty years on stage, I've never found a substitute for the excitement of entertaining with a guitar in my hand, and reaching out and touching those audiences. I enjoy travelling the world, meeting people and finding that singing and playing is a common language that gets through.

I'm often asked what made the Sixties so special, why that music has such an impact even now, and, I expect, will continue to be popular for many more years. Why will people tell their children and grandchildren about 'the good old Sixties'?

My answer is that the songs were happy, the music simple and the lyrics nice to listen to. We didn't try to change the world.

Discography

Gerry Marsden on record

UK SINGLES

CAT. NO	TITLE	RELEASED	CHART
COLUMBIA DB 4987	How Do You Do It?/Away From You	14 March 1963	1
COLUMBIA DB 7041	I Like It/It's Happened to Me	30 May 1963	1
COLUMBIA DB 7126	You'll Never Walk Alone/It's Alright	10 October 1963	1
COLUMBIA DB 7189	I'm the One/You've Got What I Like	16 January 1964	2
COLUMBIA DB 7268	Don't Let the Sun Catch You Crying/Show Me That You Care	16 April 1964	6
COLUMBIA DB 7353	It's Gonna Be Alright/It's Just Because	3 September 1964	24
COLUMBIA DB 7437	Ferry Cross the Mersey/You You You	17 December 1964	8
COLUMBIA DB 7504	I'll Be There/Baby You're So Good to Me	25 March 1965	15
COLUMBIA DB 7738	Walk Hand in Hand/Dreams	18 November 1965	29
COLUMBIA DB 7835	La La La/Without You	February 1966	
COLUMBIA DB 8044	Girl on a Swing/Fool to Myself	November 1966	
CBS 2784	Please Let Them Be/I'm Not Blue*	March 1967	
CBS 2946	Gilbert Green/What Makes You Love Me*	August 1967	
CBS 3575	Liverpool/Charlie Girl**	April 1968	
NEMS 56-3831	In the Year of April/Every Day*	November 1968	
NEMS 56-4229	Every Little Minute/In Days of Old*	May 1969	
DECCA F13172	I've Got My Ukulele/What a Day*	May 1971	

Catalog	Title	Date
PHOENIX NIX 129	Amo Credo/Come Break Bread*	April 1972
EMI 2086	You'll Never Walk Alone/How Do You Do It?/I Like It	November 1973
DJM DJS 298	Remember (The Days of Rock and Roll)/*** There's Still Time	March 1974
DJM DJS 314	They Don't Make Days Like That Any More/* Can't You Hear the Song	August 1974
DJM DJS 362	Your Song/Days I Spent with You*	April 1975
DJM DJS 10708	My Home Town/Lovely Lady*	September 1976
PENTAGON PENT 2	You'll Never Walk Alone/Here I Go Again	May 1977
EMI 2689	I Like It/How Do You Do It?/Chills	November 1977
CREOLE CR 195	You'll Never Walk Alone/Ferry Cross the Mersey	August 1979
WYND UP JB2	Ferry Cross the Mersey/Don't Let the Sun Catch You Crying	June 1980
DEB 105	Unchained Melody/Girl What You Doin'?	April 1982
DEB 107	Oh My Love/If	January 1983
DEB 111	Ferry Cross the Mersey/How Do You Do It?/I Like It	May 1983
EMI G45 25	How Do You Do It?/I Like It	May 1984
SMP SKM 8	Ferry Cross the Mersey/How Do You Do It?/I'm the One	June 1984
SPARTAN BRAD 1	You'll Never Walk Alone/Messages**** (Also on 12" as Brad 112)	June 1985
PACE 100	The Rose/You are my Everything	September 1988

PWL 41	Ferry Cross the Mersey/Abide With Me*****	May 1989	1
(7" & 12")	(by Liverpool Metropolitan Cathedral Choir)	May 1991	
GULF 1	As Time Stood Still		

This list is comprehensive but does not include re-issued hits on such labels as Past Masters, Blast From The Past, Goldens 45s, etc.

*as by Gerry Marsden
**as by Gerry Marsden and Derek Nimmo
***as by Gerry Marsden and the Pacemakers
****as by The Crowd
*****as by The Christians, Holly Johnson, Paul McCartney, Gerry Marsden and Stock Aitken Waterman

UK EPs

CAT. NO	TITLE	RELEASED	CHART
COLUMBIA SEG 8257	*How Do You Do It?* How Do You Do It?/Away From You/ I Like It/It's Happened to Me	July 1963	34
COLUMBIA SEG 8295	*You'll Never Walk Alone* You'll Never Walk Alone/Jambalaya/ Chills/A Shot of Rhythm and Blues	December 1963	
COLUMBIA SEG 8311	*I'm the One* I'm the One/You've Got What I Like/ You Can't Fool Me/Don't You Ever	February 1964	
COLUMBIA SEG 8346	*Don't Let the Sun Catch You Crying* Don't Let the Sun Catch You Crying/ Show Me That You Care/Summertime/ Where Have You Been?	May 1964	
COLUMBIA SEG 8367	*It's Gonna Be Alright* It's Gonna Be Alright/It's Just Because/ Maybellene/You're the Reason	December 1964	
COLUMBIA SEG 8388	*Gerry in California* Dizzy Miss Lizzy/My Babe/ Away from You/What'd I Say? (All recorded live)	February 1965	

COLUMBIA SEG 8397   *Ferry Cross the Mersey*   March 1965
It's Gonna Be Alright/I'll Wait for You/
Why Oh Why?/Ferry Cross the Mersey

COLUMBIA SEG 8426   *Rip It Up*   June 1965
Reelin' and Rockin'/Whole Lotta Shakin'
Goin' On/Rip It Up/You Win Again

UK LPs

CAT. NO	TITLE	RELEASED	CHART
COLUMBIA 33SX 1546 SCX 3492	*How Do You Like It?* A Shot of Rhythm and Blues/Jambalaya/ Where Have You Been?/Here's Hoping/ Pretend/Maybellene/You'll Never Walk Alone/ The Wrong Yo Yo/You're the Reason/Chills/ You Can't Fool Me/Don't You Ever/Summertime/ Slow Down	October 1963	2
REGAL STARLINE REG 1070	*You'll Never Walk Alone* (Same tracks as Columbia 33SX 1546)	1964	
COLUMBIA 33SX 1693 SCX 3544	*Ferry Cross the Mersey* It's Gonna Be Alright/Why Oh Why?/ Fall in Love/Think About Love/ This Thing Called Love/Baby You're So Good To Me/I'll Wait for You/ She's the Only Girl for Me/Ferry Cross the Mersey/plus tracks by the Fourmost, Cilla Black and the George Martin Orchestra	February 1965	19

MFP 1153	*How Do You Like It?* (Same tracks as Columbia 33SX 1546)	1967
EMI NUT 10	*The Best of Gerry and the Pacemakers* I Like It/You're the Reason/I'm the One/ It's Gonna Be Alright/Away from You/ How Do You Do It?/Walk Hand in Hand/ I'll Be There/A Shot of Rhythm and Blues/ Ferry Cross the Mersey/You'll Never Walk Alone/ Don't Let the Sun Catch You Crying/ Where Have You Been?/Think About Love/Jambalaya/ Chills/Why Oh Why?/My Babe	September 1977
PACER 001	*A Portrait of Gerry and the Pacemakers* Rock and Roll's the Music for My Soul/ I'll Be There/I'm the One/Why Do I (Love You)?/ Please Let the Sun Shine Over the Mountain/ How Do You Do It?/Girl What You Doin'?/ Ferry Cross the Mersey/Every Day/Don't Let the Sun Catch You Crying/I Like It/You'll Never Walk Alone	June 1981
THAT'S ENTERTAINMENT TERS 1028	*Pull Both Ends* 19 tracks from the musical by Gerry and The Cast	1982
DEB 1101	*Gerry and the Pacemakers* *20 Year Anniversary Album* You'll Never Walk Alone/Magic Moments/ Give Me Your Word/Ferry Cross the Mersey/	November 1982

I'll Be There/Whiter Shade of Pale/
If/Unchained Melody/Don't Let the Sun
Catch You Crying/I'll Be Home/I Like It/
Oh My Love/The Story of My Life/
How Do You Do It?/All in the Game/
World Without Love/The Minute You're Gone/
I'm the One/Where Do You Go To My Lovely?/
House of the Rising Sun

REVIVAL MEV LP 009   *Gerry and the Pacemakers*   April 1983
How Do You Do It?/Ferry Cross The Mersey/
It's Still Rock N Roll To Me/I'm the One/
Unchained Melody/Rollover Beethoven/
Imagine/Running Man/Just the Way You Are

MFP 4156541   *The Very Best of Gerry and the Pacemakers*   June 1984
How Do You Do It?/I Like It/It's Gonna Be
Alright/I'll Be There/Girl on Swing/
Come Back to Me/When Oh When?/Don't Let the
Sun Catch You Crying/You'll Never Walk Alone/
I'm the One/Walk Hand in Hand/La La La/
It's All Right/Give All Your Love to Me/
Hallelujah I Love Her So/Ferry Cross the Mersey

K TEL ONE 1274   *Lennon/McCartney Songbook*   April 1985
Mull of Kintyre/The Long and Winding Road/
Woman/It's for You/You've Got to Hide Your
Love Away/With a Little Luck/Imagine/
Pipes of Peace/Ebony and Ivory/Silly Love Songs/

163

PACER 002	Let It Be/The Fool on the Hill/My Love/(Just Like) Starting Over/Love/Yesterday *Survivor* I'm a Survivor/Story of my Life/Ferry Cross the Mersey/Why Do I?/I Like It/Unchained Melody/They Don't Make Days Like That Anymore/I'm the One/All in the Game/I'll Be There/How Do You Do It?/Give Me Your Word/Don't Let the Sun Catch You Crying/You'll Never Walk Alone	August 1985
EMI EMS 1125	*The Hit Singles Album* How Do You Do It?/Away From You/I Like It/It's Happened to Me/You'll Never Walk Alone/It's Alright/I'm the One/You've Got What I Like/Don't Let the Sun Catch You Crying/Show Me That You Care/It's Gonna Be Alright/It's Just Because/Ferry Cross the Mersey/You You You/I'll Be There/Baby You're So Good To Me	March 1986
CASTLE SHLP 102	*Ferry Cross the Mersey* (same tracks as Columbia 33SX 1693)	April 1986
PACER PAC 01	*Gerry and the Pacemakers 25th Anniversary Album* How Do You Do It?/I'll Be There/I'm the One/Ferry Cross the Mersey/Please Let the Sun Shine Over the Mountain/You'll Never Walk Alone/Don't Let the Sun Catch You Crying/All in the Game/	March 1987

SEE FOR MILES SEE 95	Oh My Love/Whiter Shade of Pale/Unchained Melody/I Like It	August 1987
	The EP Collection	
	How Do You Do It?/Away From You/I Like It/Chills/A Shot of Rhythm and Blues/You'll Never Walk Alone/You've Got What I Like/I'm the One/Don't Let the Sun Catch You Crying/Where Have You Been?/Maybellene/You're the Reason/It's Gonna Be Alright/I'll Wait for You/Ferry Cross the Mersey/You Win Again/Reelin' and Rockin'/Whole Lotta Shakin Goin On/Skinny Lizzie/My Babe/Away from You/What'd I Say?	
BGO LP 57	*How Do You Like It?*	July 1989
	(same tracks as Columbia 33SX 1546)	
PACER PACE 101	*Gerry and the Pacemakers Live*	October 1989
	How Do You Do It?/Pretend/The Rose/I'm the One/All in the Game/Chills/Don't Let the Sun Catch You Crying/It's Gonna Be Alright/Root Beer Rag/Ferry Cross the Mersey/Here's Hoping/I Saw Her Standing There/You'll Never Walk Alone/I Like It	
CASTLE CCSLP 247	*Gerry and the Pacemakers The Collection* (2 LPS)	June 1990
	Ferry Cross the Mersey/Away from You/Without You/You Win Again/Hallelujah I Love Her So/Jambalaya/I'm the One/A Shot of Rhythm and Blues/The Way You Look Tonight/Baby You're So Good to Me/You You You/Reelin' and Rockin'/How Do You Do It?/	

What'd I Say?/Chills/Show Me That You Care/
Rip It Up/You've Got What I Like/Don't Let the
Sun Catch You Crying/I'll Wait for You/Where Have
You Been?/Maybellene/You're the Reason/Whole Lott
Shakin' Goin' On

Many Gerry and the Pacemakers tracks can also be found on compilation albums such as *Hits of The Sixties, Sixties Beat, Northern Beat*, etc. etc.

US Singles

CAT. NO	TITLE	RELEASED	CHART
LAURIE 3162	How Do You Do It?/Away From You	April 1963	
LAURIE 3196	I Like It/It's Happened to Me	August 1963	
LAURIE 3218	You'll Never Walk Alone/It's Alright	January 1964	
LAURIE 3233	I'm the One/How Do You Do It?	March 1964	
LAURIE 3251	Don't Let the Sun Catch You Crying/ Away From You		
LAURIE 3261	How Do You Do It?/You'll Never Walk Alone	May 1964	4
LAURIE 3233	I'm the One/It's Alright	June 1964	9
LAURIE 3271	I Like It/Jambalaya	June 1964	82
LAURIE 3279	I'll Be There/You You You	September 1964	17
LAURIE 3284	Ferry Cross the Mersey/Pretend	November 1964	14
LAURIE 3293	It's Gonna Be Alright/Skinny Minnie	January 1965	6
LAURIE 3302	You'll Never Walk Alone/Away from You	March 1965	23
LAURIE 3313	Give All Your Love to Me/You're the Reason	May 1965	48
LAURIE 3323	Walk Hand in Hand/Dreams	July 1965	
LAURIE 3337	La La La/Without You	November 1965	
LAURIE 3354	Girl on a Swing/The Way You Look Tonight	March 1966	
LAURIE 3370	Looking for my Life/The Big Bright Green Pleasure Machine	August 1966	
		January 1967	

| COLUMBIA 4–44309 | Gilbert Green/Please Let Them Be* | August 1967 |
| LAURIE 3251 | Don't Let the Sun Catch You Crying/ Away From You | November 1970 |

This list does not include re-issued hits on such labels as Eric, etc.

*as by Gerry Marsden

US LPs

CAT. NO	TITLE	RELEASED	CHART
LAURIE LLP 2024 SLP 2024 CAPITOL T-90555 DT-90555	*Don't Let the Sun Catch You Crying* Don't Let the Sun Catch You Crying/ I'm the One/Away From You/Jambalaya/ Maybellene/You'll Never Walk Alone/ How Do You Do It?/You're the Reason/ Don't You Ever/Summertime/Slow Down/ Show Me That You Care	June 1964	29
CAPITOL LLP 2027 SLP 2027 CAPITOL T 90460 ST 90460	*Second Album* I Like It/A Shot of Rhythm and Blues/ Where Have You Been/Here's Hoping/Pretend/ The Wrong Yo Yo/Chills/You Can't Fool Me/ It's Happened to Me/It's Alright/Slow Down/ Jambalaya	October 1964	129
LAURIE LLP 2030 SLP 2030 CAPITOL T-90385 ST-90385	*I'll Be There* I'll Be There/What'd I Say?/Rip It Up/ You Win Again/You You You/Now I'm Alone/ My Babe/Reelin and Rockin/I Count the Tears/ Whole Lotta Shakin Goin On/It'll Be Me/ Skinny Minnie	January 1965	120

UNITED ARTISTS UAL 3387 UAS 6387 CAPITOL T-90812 ST-90812	*'Ferry Cross the Mersey'* Ferry Cross the Mersey/It's Gonna Be Alright/Why Oh Why?/Fall in Love/Think About Love/This Thing Called Love/Baby You're So Good to Me/I'll Wait for You/She's the Only Girl for Me, plus three tracks by other artists	February 1965	13
LAURIE LLP 2031 SLP 2031 CAPITOL T-90384 ST-90384	*Greatest Hits* Ferry Cross the Mersey/How Do You Do It?/I'm the One/My Babe/Away from You/I'll Be There/It's Gonna Be Alright/Pretend/I Like It/Chills/It'll Be Me/Don't Let the Sun Catch You Crying	May 1965	44
LAURIE LLP 2037 SLP 2037	*Girl on a Swing* Girl on a Swing/The Way You Look Tonight/Guantanamera/Pretty Flamingo/At the End of a Rainbow/Looking for My Life/The Big Bright Green Pleasure Machine/See You in September/Who Can I Turn To?/Without You/Strangers in the Night/La La La	November 1966	
CAPITOL SM-11898	*The Best of Gerry and the Pacemakers* I Like It/I'm the One/It's Gonna Be Alright/Away From You/How Do You Do It?/Walk Hand in Hand/Ferry Cross the Mersey/You'll Never Walk Alone/Don't Let the Sun Catch You Crying/Chills	February 1979	
ACCORD SN 7148	*Ferry Cross the Mersey* Ferry Cross the Mersey/How Do You Do It?/Ferry Cross the Mersey/	October 1981	

It's Still Rock and Roll to Me/I'm the One/
Unchained Melody/Roll Over Beethoven/Imagine/
Running Man/Just the Way You Are

Many Gerry and the Pacemaker tracks can be found on compilation albums such as *British Airwaves*, etc.

UK CDs

CAT. NO	TITLE	RELEASED	CHART
EMI CDP 746	*Hit Singles Plus* (same tracks as EMS 1125)	June 1987	
SEE FOR MILES SEE CD 95	*EP Collection* (same as tracks on LP SEE 95)	July 1989	
PACED 101	*Gerry and the Pacemakers Live* (same tracks as LP PACE 101)	October 1989	
CASTLE CCSCD 247	*The Collection* (same tracks as Castle CCSLP 247)	June 1990	
THAT'S POP TPOO8	*Greatest Hits* How Do You Do It?/I'm the One/Ferry Cross the Mersey/It's Still Rock and Roll to Me/ Roll Over Beethoven/Unchained Melody/ Imagine/Running Man/Just The Way You Are	1991	
OBJECT ORO 144	*Ferry Cross the Mersey* (same tracks as above)	1991	
EMI CDP 7 99030 2	*The EMI Years: The Best of Gerry and the Pacemakers* How Do You Do It?/Maybellene/I Like It/Chills/ Pretend/Jambalaya/You're the Reason/Hello Little Girl/ You'll Never Walk Alone/A Shot of Rhythm and Blues/	April 1992	

US CDs

Slow Down/It's All Right/I'm the One/Don't Let the Sun Catch You Crying/You've Got What I Like/It's Just Because/You You You/It's Gonna Be Alright/Ferry Cross the Mersey/I'll Wait for You/Hallelujah I Love Her So/Reelin' and Rockin'/Why Oh Why?/Baby You're So Good to Me/Walk Hand in Hand/Dreams/Give All Your Love to Me/I'll Be There/La La La/Fool to Myself/Girl on A Swing

UNITED ARTISTS
CDP 7–96093–2

The Legends of Rock and Roll

The Best of Gerry and the Pacemakers
The Definitive Collection
How Do You Do It?/Away From You/I Like It/It's Happened to Me/Pretend/Hello Little Girl/You'll Never Walk Alone/It's Alright/You're the Reason/I'm the One/You've Got What I Like/Don't Let the Sun Catch You Crying/Show Me That You Care/It's Gonna Be Alright/It's Just Because/Ferry Cross the Mersey/You You You/I'll Wait for You/I'll Be There/Give All Your Love to Me/Walk Hand in Hand/Dreams/La La La/Girl on a Swing/Fool to Myself

Many Gerry and the Pacemakers tracks can be found on CD compilations.

Songs Written and Recorded by Gerry Marsden

Away From You
Baby You're So Good to Me
Come Back to Me
Come Break Bread
Days I Spent with You
Don't Let the Sun Catch You Crying
Don't You Ever
Dreams
Every Day is Just Another Day
Every Little Minute
Fall in Love
Ferry Cross the Mersey
Fool to Myself
Girl What You Doin'?
Give All Your Love to Me
I'll Wait for You
I'm Not Blue
I'm the One
In Days of Old
It's Alright
It's Gonna Be Alright

It's Happened to Me
It's Just Because
La La La
Lovely Lady
Now I'm Alone
Please Let the Sun Shine Over the Mountain
Prove It*
She's the Only Girl for Me
Show Me That You Care
Think About Love
This Thing Called Love
What Makes Me Love You?
When Oh When?
Why Do I (Love You)?
Why Oh Why?
Without You
You are My Everything
You've Got What I Like
You You You

*This song recorded by Tommy Quickly

Index

INDEX